EUROPEAN YEARBOOK OF
BUSINESS HISTORY

EUROPEAN YEARBOOK OF BUSINESS HISTORY

Editors
Terry Gourvish   Business History Unit, London School of Economics
                        Houghton Street, London WC2A 2AE

Editorial staff:
Jane Waller   Deputy Archivist, ING Barings
Andrea H. Schneider   Association for Business History e.V.

Edited in association with:
Harold James   Princeton University
Geoffrey Jones   University of Reading
Akira Kudo   University of Tokyo
Alain Plessis   University of Paris
Manfred Pohl   Historical Institute, Deutsche Bank AG, Frankfurt
Gabriel Tortella   University of Madrid
Herman Van der Wee   Leuven University
Mira Wilkins   Florida University
Vera Zamagni   University of Bologna

NOTES FOR CONTRIBUTORS: *The European Yearbook of Business History* is an annual publication of the Society for European History - SEBH e.V. The journal is concerned with the history of individual European enterprises and entrepreneurs, as well as multinational corporations, and will also publish new research and surveys in the wider field of business history. The journal aims to cover all Europe, not just those countries of the European Union, during, but not exclusively, the nineteenth and twentieth centuries.

Prospective contributors should contact the SEBH office (see address below) for guidelines on producing contributions for the *Yearbook*. All contributions will be refered. Research articles should normally be of 10,000 words including foot-notes, whereas surveys should be shorter at 5,000 words. Contributions should be sent as hard copy and on disk, or as e-mail attachment to:
Society for European Business History –
SEBH e.V.
Zimmerweg 6, D-60325 Frankfurt am Main
Tel.: + 49 69 7103 5993/4; fax: +49 69 9720 3308
E-mail: schneider@businesshistory.de

SUBSCRIPTIONS: *The European Yearbook of Business History* is published annually. A subscription to the *Yearbook* costs £50, including postage. Orders should be sent to your usual bookseller or subscription agent, or direct to Customer Services, Ashgate Publishing Ltd, Gower House, Croft Road, Aldershot, Hampshire, GU11 3HR; tel. +44 (0)1252 317707; fax +44 (0)1252 343151.

PERMISSIONS: Requests for permission to re-use material published in the journal should be sent to Ashgate Publishing Ltd, Gower House, Croft Road, Aldershot, Hampshire GU11 3HR.

European Yearbook of Business History

Vol. 3, 2000

edited by
Terry Gourvish

Published by ROUTLEDGE on behalf of the
Society for European Business History

First published 2000 by Ashgate Publishing

Reissued 2018 by Routledge
2 Park Square, Milton Park, Abingdon, Oxon OX14 4RN
711 Third Avenue, New York, NY 10017, USA

Routledge is an imprint of the Taylor & Francis Group, an informa business

Publisher's Note
The publisher has gone to great lengths to ensure the quality of this reprint but points out that some imperfections in the original copies may be apparent.

Disclaimer
The publisher has made every effort to trace copyright holders and welcomes correspondence from those they have been unable to contact.

Typeset by Manton Typesetters, Louth, Lincolnshire, UK.

ISBN 13: 978-1-138-63583-8 (hbk)
ISBN 13: 978-1-138-63584-5 (pbk)
ISBN 13: 978-1-315-20403-1 (ebk)
ISSN 1462–186X

Contents

The European Yearbook of Business History

The aim of the *Yearbook* is to reflect the changing structure, experience and aspirations of European business as it approaches the Millenium. The challenge of globalization, co-operation within a single European market, and an increasing interest in corporate governance and environmental issues are illustrative of the changes which not only affect contemporary business enterprises, but also stimulate new types of scholarship among European business historians, and encourage new preservation strategies by business archivists. Increasingly, an interest in single industries in one country is being replaced by comparative analysis embracing several countries, whilst the definition of 'business history' has widened to embrace social and political issues.

The *Yearbook* intends to exploit these changes by serving as a forum for debate in Europe. It publishes new academic research on any aspect of European business history, but with special emphasis on works of synthesis, comparative studies of business activity, and reviews of current research work in individual countries, including assessments of major source materials and archives. At the same time, theoretical contributions are also welcome, as are extra-European perspectives on Europe, particularly from the United States and Japan. Published in English, the *Yearbook* aims to bring work on individual countries to a wider, European audience.

The Society for European Business History

The Society is based at the Centre for European Business History in Frankfurt am Main, Germany. It is generously supported by European companies. The Society aims to promote all aspects of European business history.

Office
Roberta Sneider
Secretary General

Marion Hausmann
Assistant

Society for European Business History e.V. – SEBH
Zimmerweg 6
D-60325 Frankfurt am Main
Germany

Tel.: +49 69 7103 5993/4
Fax: +49 69 9720 3308
E-mail: Roberta.Sneider@banking history.de
        bekassel@businesshistory.de
Homepage: www.businesshistory.de

Details of membership can be obtained from the Society at the above
address.

Divide and Rule: Regulation and Response in the Port Wine Trade 1812–40*

Paul Duguid, University of California, Berkeley
Teresa Silva Lopes, University of Reading and Universidade Católica Portuguesa

INTRODUCTION

Recent fruitful discussions in business history from the perspective of institutional economics have, among other things, indicated the importance of historical studies of the forms and functions of regulation. Such studies can provide empirical support for, or alternatively challenge, institutional and regulation theories. To this end, this paper investigates state regulation in the port wine trade in the decades following the Napoleonic wars (1812–40) and the response of port wine traders.[1]

The period and place seem apt for the topic of regulation and the response of regulated firms because they embrace the decline of the *ancien regime* and the rise of liberalism in Portugal. Thus they bring face to face mercantilist regulation and mercantile aspirations for free trade. The wine trade, for its part, provides a useful subject for such a study. Because bulk trade in wine was relatively easy to regulate, the wine trade has a long history of regulation, at the point both of production and consumption. The port trade, moreover, is particularly interesting. In the mid-eighteenth century, the Portuguese established the world's first significant wine demarcation over an area whose wine, fortified with brandy, had found particular favour in the British market.[2] Thus a form of regulation through demarcation was established that has been followed subsequently by all major wine regions.[3] The early nineteenth century port trade offers an opportunity to understand how regulation worked historically, whom it affected, what effects it produced, and what happened when it disappeared.

It seems almost banal to begin with the assumption that the port merchants, as members of a fraternity of free traders, would oppose regulation.[4] Undoubtedly, the Portuguese regulations annoyed the British and they reacted as might be expected. British merchants protested to consuls, wrote to the Board of Trade, petitioned parliament, and published pamphlets. The public and published record of this dissent is unavoidable.[5] Yet, in this façade of vociferous unanimity are some surprising cracks. A couple of pamphleteering port merchants of the period, for example, could not agree on which regulation was the most detrimental. One insisted that it was the tax on consumption. His opponent had no doubt it was the control of production.[6] Elsewhere in the Portuguese wine trade, a Madeira merchant, who would undoubtedly have known of the port regulations, rather surprisingly wrote to his correspondent on the island encouraging regulation, 'you must for your own sakes & that of the Island in general get the Legislature of your Government to prevent the introduction of such damned trash of Brandy or you will lose a great deal of business & the Island a great deal of Character, which will soon go, & it be not supported by a real superiority of quality'.[7] Later, a port merchant, contemplating the possible demise of that trade's regulatory body at the hands of the new liberal parliament wrote to one of his correspondents, 'people do not readily reconcile themselves to its being done away with and many of the English Houses even, are doubtful how far their interests would benefit by such a step'. More generally, many of the protests give a sense as much of ritual as of genuine rancour.[8]

At this point, it is worth remembering a wise comment by Ronald Coase: 'The eloquence and force of Adam Smith's denunciation of regulation designed to narrow the competition seems to have blinded us to the fact that dealers also have an interest in making regulations which widen the market'.[9] Few traders have been as eloquent as Adam Smith, but many were more belligerent. And inevitably some sought to use regulation to widen their markets by narrowing competition. Their public statements may thus blind historians to the inconsistencies which appear when statements are matched to behaviour, for merchants were evidently not universally opposed to regulation, nor did they universally suffer at its hands. Undoubtedly they often resented intervention when it was in place. But often, too, they called for it when it was not, understandably seeking the advantages of both protection and free trade without the disadvantages of either.

The challenge for the historian, then, is to get behind the public pronouncements and posturing to understand how people actually behaved in practice. And here, as we try to show, the business historian has the advantage of being equipped to consider not only the letters, protests, and publications, but also financial statements and business practices. The latter can helpfully reveal the underlying interests and strategies that other records may willfully conceal. In its exploration of the reconstruction of the British port trade after Napoleon's continental blockade, this paper sets out to understand both regulation and the business strategies and

practices of the regulated. In search of the former, it considers the role of
the Portuguese regulatory body, and in search of the actual rather than
espoused attitudes of the latter, it looks at their reactions as they appear in
business records, not just in their public, comments. Businessmen, like
everyone else, after all, often find it advantageous to say one thing but to
do another.[11]

The port merchants may also provide a useful window onto British
merchants of the period more generally. Our study reflects Chapman's
contention that the Napoleonic wars mark a turning point in the history of
British merchants and shows how conditions changed for those who survived.[12] In the post-war port trade, the old verities on which old firms had
depended – steady profits, substantial capital, avoidance of debt, and
(despite their protests) predictable regulation – no longer assured stability
and control. In these conditions, a new breed of merchants willing to take
greater risks was emerging, and in the port trade at least, these merchants
rose to dominate the trade.

To make this case, we begin by outlining the regulatory history of the
port trade, before turning to concentrate on the return of the British to a
trade in which they had long been involved but from which they had been
all but excluded for most of Napoleon's continental blockade (1806–12)
and his frequent invasions of Portugal. We introduce a group of traders,
divided between those returning to the trade and those arriving for the
first time. We explain the financial problems that afflicted all in this group,
beset as they were by falling profits, inadequate capital, and rising debt in
a period of economic contraction and poor wine. We then turn to the
Portuguese regulatory body and its attempts to stabilise this increasingly
unstable trade through regulation. Our sample of firms then allows us to
gauge the responses to this regulation. In their responses, we argue, the
new firms pursued more aggressive, risk-taking policies than the old and in
doing so became the most powerful exporters. We conclude that the
strategies of these firms helped establish the patterns of the trade in the
free-market era, patterns that are easily attributed to the institutions of the
free market, but which, in fact, continued to reflect prior regulation.

HISTORY OF THE TRADE

British trade (and probably the wine trade) with Portugal goes back as far,
at least, as the Treaty of Windsor (1386). British merchants began to
export wine from the Douro river through the city of Oporto, which
stands at the river's estuary, from the mid-seventeenth century, when they
formed themselves into a 'factory', a group of merchants collectively ceded
certain privileges by the Portuguese government.[13] British wars with France,
increasing the importance of Portuguese wine, expanded this trade, and

the Methuen treaty of 1703 cemented it. The 1740s, however, saw a slump and, as a result, rising tension between British exporters and Portuguese brokers and farmers.[14] By 1755, the autocratic Portuguese prime minister (the future Marquis Pombal, so known by that name) decided that the state should intervene in this dispute, in good part no doubt because he sought the income a well-regulated trade could provide, and after the Lisbon earthquake such income was desperately needed.[15]

To this end, Pombal created the *Companhia Geral da Agricultura das Vinhas do Alto Douro* (the General Company for the Cultivation of the Vines of the Upper Douro, hereafter, the Companhia). A joint-stock enterprise, the *Companhia* was given the power to regulate production, sales and price, transportation, storage, domestic retail trade, and export of wines from the Douro region, which in the following years was carefully demarcated and mapped in an annual cadastre. Each year, the *Companhia* decided, farmer by farmer, what wine was sufficient for the British market. It denominated such wine *legal* – legally exportable to Britain. Less good wine it qualified as *separado*, and set it aside for the rest of Europe and Brazil.[16] Then, at the annual spring wine fair, which it also oversaw, it set the price range for each category, recorded all contracts, and supervised the transportation of wine from farmers in the country to merchants in the city.

Under the vigilant eye of the Marquis, the *Companhia* used these controls to establish a careful and calculated balance among the divided interests of farmers, Portuguese merchants, and foreign (predominantly British) exporters.[17] Understandably, all these constituents disliked the new restraints, but the *Companhia's* approach of divide and rule prevented any concerted opposition. The Portuguese government generally dismissed the protests that the British sent to Lisbon and London, though intermittently the *Companhia* made individual protesters and their businesses feel its displeasure. The *Companhia* responded decisively, however, to internal dissent, acting swiftly against forestalling by brokers and responding savagely following anti-*Companhia* riots in Oporto.[18]

With Pombal's fall in 1777, the *Companhia* was slowly transformed into something a little kinder, gentler, certainly weaker, and better disposed towards the British and to free trade than the stern Pombaline institution that had ruled over imprisonment, exile and, indirectly, even execution.[19] The effects on the trade, however, are curious. The British had claimed that an apparent fall in the number of British houses 'may be referred to the many Alarms and vexations occasioned by the Institution of the Wine Company'.[20] This claim would suggest that, with a less-vexatious and better-disposed *Companhia*, new firms would be willing to enter the market. But this did not happen. Rather, in the post-Pombaline years, while the lucrative British trade expanded, producing what has been called port wine's 'golden age', that trade became concentrated in increasingly fewer hands.[21] The number of British exporters sank from forty-seven in 1771 to twenty-two in 1786, while the British share (by volume) of the lucrative British market rose to 86 per cent, with ten British firms controlling 70 per cent of that trade.[22]

While a weaker *Companhia* did not noticeably increase competition among the exporters, it does seem to have produced an efficient market among the farmers, despite fixing the price at which wine could be sold. Had that market not been efficient, almost inevitably the exporters would have tried to exert more control over wine production – either by engaging in long-term contracts with farmers or by buying land in the Douro to produce wine. In fact, neither happened to any great extent. Before the Napoleonic wars, there was some long-term contracting, but firms in general seem to have disliked it and preferred to buy each year in an open market.[23] Records for Offley, one of the firms we discuss below, suggest that before the Napoleonic wars the majority of its suppliers in any one year had not sold to the company before. More reliable data for the period between the Napoleonic wars and the Civil War indicate that two-thirds of the same firm's suppliers (some 300 farmers in all) sold to Offley in one year only, and only 6 per cent sold in five or more years. Similarly, few firms owned property in the Douro, and those that did produced little wine in relation to their total production. Offley had a small holding, but the wine produced there was generally of too poor a quality to qualify for the British market. Only after the collapse of the *Companhia* is there significant evidence of contracting and land ownership, indicating that in the absence of the *Companhia's* regulation, pressure for backward integration must have grown.[24]

The *Companhia's* strategy of control, then, apparently took different forms. In Oporto, it seems to have tolerated the formation of an oligarchy of British exporters. In the Douro, it promoted competition among the farmers. And in between the two, the *Companhia* acted to restrain forestalling by the Portuguese merchants who brokered wine between the farmers and exporters. The *Companhia* made a good deal of money by brokering such wine itself, so it had a strong interest in suppressing this competition. In all, the *Companhia* seems to have sought a balance of power between these three parties – farmers, exporters, and brokers – so that, by dividing them, it could rule them.

If the thus-tolerated British oligarchy became complaisant, the Napoleonic wars, a 'major watershed' as Chapman notes for all traders, must have proved a severe jolt. At first, with British ships risking capture at sea, the Portuguese took over much of the shipping trade. Then, after the 'continental blockade' set in and closed European ports to the British, the Portuguese increasingly ran not just the shipping, but the export trade itself. The British merchants, meanwhile, were forced to take their goods, their capital, and their persons to Britain. This, we suggest, was a significant moment in the history of the firms, for in the years after the war, the people proved more ready to return than their capital. Yet capital was a key element in the oligarchy's arsenal. The same Consul who claimed the *Companhia* inhibited competition was forced to concede that there was also 'a disinclination for the establishment of new Houses in a commerce where very large Capitals are required.' Returning with far less capital than they left with, the old firms found several new houses willing to establish themselves in competition.[25]

A slice of the trade

The central focus of this paper is the return of this trade to British control in the post-war years, which were also the last years of the regulatory *Companhia*. This was abolished in 1834, following the Liberal victory in the Portuguese Civil War of 1828–34.[26] We rely on export records, which reveal the number of firms and annual exports of each. But we also draw on the surviving financial records of a handful of firms. These, as Table 1 reveals, divide into two groups. Four existed before the *Companhia*. A fifth, Swann Knowsley can be traced back at least to 1763. These five pre-Napoleonic War firms we call 'the old guard'. They formed a significant part of the pre-war oligarchy. The remaining three, which we call newcomers, are not only post-Pombaline, but predominantly post the Napoleonic wars.[27] This distinction allows us to compare the strategies of the old and the new and to view not only entries (evident in the new), but also exits, as Swann Knowsley went out of business in 1830 and Campbell liquidated its assets in 1824, leaving the trade to Joseph Taylor, the junior partner.[28]

Table 1: Sample of new and old firms in the post-war trade in port[29]

Firm	Date founded in Oporto
Old guard	
Campbell, Bowden, Gray, Camo, Taylor	1692
Croft & Co	1678
Hunt, Newman, Roope	1735
Offley, Forrester, Webber	1730
Swann Knowsley/Sobral Pinto	1763
Newcomers	
Martinez, Jones, Gassiot	1809 and 1834
Sandeman & Co	1814
Cockburn, Wauchope, Moodie, Greg	1815

Table 2: Ranking in list of exporters compared to other British firms and to all firms, with per cent market share (by volume)

Firms	1812 Ranking British	1812 Ranking All	1812 Market share (%)	1820 Ranking British	1820 Ranking All	1820 Market Share (%)	1832 Ranking British	1832 Ranking All	1832 Market Share (%)
Old guard									
Campbell/Taylor†	5	16	(2.2)	13	24	(1.4)	10	16	(1.5)
Croft	3	11	(2.9)	3	5	(4.0)	4	4	(6.5)
Hunt	12	37	(0.1)	14	25	(1.3)	14	28	(1.1)
Offley	2	8	(3.6)	7	10	(3.0)	2	2	(8.5)
Swann Knowsley	11	35	(0.1)	10	14	(2.4)	n/a	n/a	n/a
Newcomers									
Martinez	n/a	n/a	n/a	n/a	n/a	n/a	n/a	n/a	n/a
Sandeman	n/a	n/a	n/a	8	11	(2.8)	1	1	(8.7)
Cockburn	n/a	n/a	n/a	16	31	(1.0)	8	10	(3.8)
Number of equivalent firms (1/H)	12	16		24	24		32	23	
Number of firms		50			87			83	

* % Share – represents the exports of the firm relative to the exports for the sector in each period
† By 1832, the firm of Campbell had been replaced by the firm of Taylor
n/a = not applicable

Our group is not representative of the sector as a whole. Since the war began, for instance, there had been many more Portuguese than English firms in the trade, and this predominance held in the post-war years. Moreover, all our firms generally performed well above the average for the trade. They probably do, however, offer a cross-section of the British firms. Table 2 shows how they ranked against their British competitors and in the sector as a whole in the post-war years.

As Table 2 also shows, the old firms faced some difficulty re-establishing their dominance in the trade from which they had been expelled by the continental blockade and French invasions during the Napoleonic wars. By 1812 only twelve British firms had returned and Offley, before the war the dominant private exporter, now ranked only eight in the sector (although it was the second most important British firm).[31] In this year there were fifty firms exporting but, as indicated by the index of the number of equivalent firms (determined as the inverse of the Herfindahl index [H], a measure of sector concentration frequently used in industrial economics), the trade was effectively run by sixteen companies. Over time, there was an increase in the number of exporting firms but the industry remained concentrated and the British returned to dominance. By 1832, despite the number of exporters growing to eighty-three, twenty-three firms effectively controlled the sector.

The post-war years

This return to dominance, however, was not preordained. The British faced a hard climb back. The pre-war withdrawal (principally between 1804 and 1807) marked a clear end to the golden age. Export volumes peaked in 1802, while prices were rising (and continued to rise to 1811). The post-war years, 1812 and beyond, were quite different. Where in the first decade of the century exports averaged 44,000 pipes per year, for the second, the figure was not quite 24,000. In 1811, exports reached their lowest level for almost 50 years. The British portion, moreover, was only seven per cent, far below the 86 per cent it achieved at the height of the golden age. That year, too, the price of wine began a steady, 40-year decline.[32]

Conditions in both Britain and Portugal precipitated the slump which the returning firms encountered. In Britain the economic boom brought on by war collapsed with peace. As one correspondent wrote:

> Numberless people who were differently employed during the War are now without the means of living as they used to do & wine is one of the expences they can best dispence with. Spirits are now to be bought from smugglers at a price equal to the duty only, & it is supposed that drinking Grog is as cheap as wine would be at 1/6 p Bottle.[33]

Meanwhile, in Portugal, the removal of the Court to Brazil in 1807 and the subsequent loss of control of the Brazil trade in 1810 brought both political and financial uncertainty. Then between 1816 and 1819 the Douro suffered a run of awful harvests. The old guard, furthermore, faced this wretched market in conditions of increasing competition. Where there were 45 exporters (of all nationalities) in 1786; there were 98 in 1816. Volatility accompanied this competition. Where 1816 produced a peak in the annual number of entries (twenty) into the trade, 1817 produced a peak in the number of exits (fourteen). Given that capital had previously both kept competition at bay and ensured stability, it is not surprising to see this new instability reflected in the financial statements and capital accounts of the post-war years.

Business of the day, as Neal points out, was funded principally through retained profits, partner's capital, and the common forms of debt available at that time. Examining each of these in turn helps to illustrate the health of the firm, their options, and their emerging strategies.[34]

Falling profits

Before the war profits had been very healthy, and because firms retained them over long periods, they provided significant fuel for growth. Between 1776 and 1779, Hunt gave its partners a return of 46 per cent, or just over 13 per cent per year compounded, on their initial investment. Offley's partners' returns over the long run, though harder to calibrate exactly, look similar.[35] The war then produced a speculative boom for those that could continue trading (primarily by putting their assets in foreign hands).

Table 3: Average annual distribution of profits (*mil reis*)[37]

Firm	War end 1810–11	Post-war 1812–20	Recovery 1821–34
Campbell	79,200	7,422	3,750
Croft	n/a	0	22,607
Hunt	74,080	15,183	[-]
Offley	n/a	3,453	33,221
Swann	n/a	22,649	[-]
Martinez	[-]	[-]	−4,754
Sandeman	n/a	3,054	33,551
Cockburn	[-]	3,100	15,000

n/a= not applicable; [-] = not available

But that boom, in which annual returns on capital reached 100 per cent, collapsed very quickly. For the group as a whole, the rate of return on capital invested for the period 1812–20 was about seven per cent, dangerously low for a trade where returns, however high, were long in coming.[36] As Table 3 shows, for the period 1812–20, Campbell's gross annual dividends were less than ten per cent of returns in the war years. Hunt, another wartime speculator, saw its distributions fall to one-fifth of their wartime level and quickly found itself relying on its non-wine trade (principally fish) to generate any profit at all. Croft (where a partner slowly withdrew his capital) paid no dividend in the period, while the venerable Offley's sank to the level of the neophytes Sandeman and Cockburn. Only Swann, which had a good portion of Portuguese (rather than British) capital in its account and was managed by the Portuguese partners, generated impressive rate of returns for its investors.

Capital shortages

Inevitably, poor profits failed to attract capital, which, as we have suggested, was a key part of the old guard's strategy. The wine business was particularly capital-intensive. The product was expensive and had to be held for the process of maturing, blending, and shipping.[38] Suppliers expected quick and even advance payments – and the *Companhia* generally saw that suppliers were paid. Customers, by comparison, were often slow to pay. Moreover, the trade was subject, even in its golden period to wild swings, but the large capital on which the houses depended helped to dampen these.

In the pre-war years, the total capital (including retained profits) credited to the partners' accounts in Offley's balance sheet reached a high of 426,502 *mil reis* (about £112,700) in 1790 (allowing the firm to export almost 6,000 pipes in a single year), following a low of 285,120 *mil reis* (about £75,000) in 1783. The post-war years look remarkably bleak by comparison. In 1812, the firm recapitalised tentatively, starting with only 109,000 *mil reis* (£25,000). Immediate losses drew that down to 74,250 *mil reis* by the end of its first year's trading, so that in 1812 and 1813 partners had to contribute another 50,000 *mil reis* to keep the books in balance. For 1812–20, its capital account averaged about 70,000 *mil reis*, barely a quarter of the pre-war low.

No doubt buoyed by its wartime profits, Hunt evidently did find adequate capital for its post-war business. In 1812, it began a partnership with 140,000 *mil reis* and in 1816 raised this to 200,000. This sum, however, also had to cover its business in fish, which was larger than its trade in wine. Hunt may have raised the additional capital, moreover, in acts of faith and hope rather than in response to its actual earnings outlook. Significantly, the existing partners failed to persuade those who knew the business best to join in this act of faith. Two partners of the London house refused to join them, saying the returns seemed insufficient for the risk.[39]

Such defections reflected the trade more generally, in the post-war years. Though most of the prominent firms returned, many prominent partners did not. Babbington, Pennell, Stafford, Stevenson, and Thompson – names famous in Oporto partnerships for decades – disappeared. Their absence signals the failure of capital to return to the trade even when firms did. In our group, the firm of Croft not only had to return without Thompson, a long-time partner, but also immediately faced the loss of another partner, Fred Croft, who slowly drained his capital from the firm in the post war years, driving the firm into debt.

The threat of debt

In the absence of profits and capital, debt became the primary option for finance. The exporters, however, turned to this with reluctance. Merchants everywhere were averse to debt, but the port merchants feared it more than most.[40] Part of this fear would have come from the wine business in England, which was notoriously weak and pyramids of debt, hollow at the core, often collapsed. The London partners who, as we mentioned earlier, rejected Hunt's Oporto venture specifically 'begged to decline taking any risk of Debts of the Wine Houses, as they think the business too precarious and the bad debts had run away with most of the Agency'. The same writer conveyed a friend's opinion that wine merchants were, 'without exception the most rotten set in London and that he would not trust one out of ten'.[41] Such fears were well-based. The old guard in particular would easily remember the early years of the war when houses, locked together in debt, had fallen like dominos as the capital supporting it dried up. Offley would have been particularly sensitive, as in 1793 one partner, unable to get his cash out of the firm expeditiously, had, when called to account by creditors, hanged himself.

In Portugal, fear of debt was equally strong. The British feared in particular the weak protection that Portuguese law provided for creditors. As one merchant wrote, 'the recovery of debts in this country is very precarious and the laws are so badly administered that a Bankrupt may with impunity defraud his creditors'.[42] Again the fears were well founded. In the post-war years, houses struggled with debt and creditors, as insolvency proved indifferent to youth or age. In 1816, Samuel Weaver, a member of the old guard, went under (leaving Croft holding wine that it did not necessarily want as security). In 1819, another old firm, Burmester called in its creditors. In 1821, Hely, a new firm, in 1822, Page Noble, an old, both failed to make payments. 1824 saw a new (Hudson) and an old (Snow) go under. Throughout this period, Warre a venerable firm, powerhouse of the pre-war years, but self-proclaimed 'general trader', stayed away from the port trade and made its money elsewhere.[43]

Here, our group proves representative. Martinez pulled out in 1816 and, as we have noted, did not return until 1834. Then in 1820, Campbell's profits stagnated, and though one of the oldest of the old, the firm collapsed into the arms of its junior partner in 1824. The other partners fled the business. And Hunt, finding itself sinking into debt in 1820, pulled out of the trade, like Warre, doing little business in wine and concentrating on fish for the period 1820–25. Both Offley and Croft struggled to balance their accounts. Offley called for more capital in a couple of years. Croft borrowed £12,000 from its senior partner and a further £18,000 from the VanZeller, a prominent Oporto house of Dutch origin.[44]

In all, then, the post-war return was a remarkably difficult time for the British traders. Stagnation, poor harvests, and weak finances beset them all. And yet, as Tables 2 and 3 suggest, not only did Hunt and Martinez return but so did solvency, so did profits, and so did British dominance. By 1840, the British held 15 of the top 20 export positions and two-thirds of the total export trade, as the Portuguese competition faded away.

How can this be explained? Good harvests no doubt account for some of this. The years 1820 and 1821 were exceptional. But good harvests after a series of poor years could bring as much harm as good, for they devalued the stock on hand making it harder to find cash or space for the new. Good strategy, perhaps – but as we will see, not necessarily the conventional old-guard strategies. And good regulation? The *Companhia's* contribution offers another possible explanation, but in this period its most visible act seems to have been to decline and fall. It was first threatened in 1821 with the appearance of a liberal parliament, and finally fell at the hands of the liberal victors of the Civil War in 1834. Nevertheless, to weigh these options, we do need to turn to the role of the *Companhia* in this period, which so far we have neglected.

The Companhia in the post-war years

The post-war years brought the Companhia troubles of its own. In 1810, to the disgust of many in Portugal, the government signed a free-trade treaty with Great Britain. This outlawed both factories and monopolies. The British factory in Oporto was dominated by wine traders. In 1788, John Croft, partner in the port house and propagandist of the British port trade, had argued that the factory made a signal contribution to the trade.[45] Nonetheless, members were forced to yield their factory privileges. They failed, however, to balance the ledger, for no one accepted their argument that the *Companhia* was a monopoly. Despite an outburst of pamphleteering, it survived.[46] The treaty, the traders' fulminations, and the need to restore the trade after the war, however, persuaded the

Companhia to act circumspectly. It remained cautious in 1815 as its charter was reconsidered. It survived this test, prorogued for twenty years. But in 1821, the liberal parliament opened the *Companhia* for scrutiny once again.

To survive again, the *Companhia* had to prove its worth and, above all, to deal with the mounting crisis in the trade, for it habitually justified itself in terms of its ability to resolve just such crises. It faced, as we have seen, low consumption, overproduction, poor quality, and growing insolvency. In the Douro, farmers complained that, unable to sell the poor wine of previous years they lacked money to harvest the wine, whatever its quality promised to be. In Oporto, the merchants were similarly unable to liquidate their old stocks to take advantage of the new or provide loans to suppliers. As a consequence, not only were British houses failing, so were the Portuguese. In the period from 1812–20, some 13 Portuguese firms exporting 200 or more pipes per annum went out of business.[47]

The *Companhia's* response reflects its old divide-and-rule strategy, giving solace to all, but dominance to none, while dividing interests to prevent alliances forming against its rule. To follow this difficult feat, we need to remember the *Companhia's* process of 'qualification' or 'separation', whereby it qualified some wine for the British market, while deeming other wine adequate only for the markets of Brazil and northern Europe.[48]

For the fair of 1821, which sold the wine harvested in 1820, the *Companhia* acted to spread the potential wealth of that remarkable vintage more evenly than in previous years. Instead of qualifying some farmers' wine as *legal* and others' as *separado*, it divided almost everyone's wine between the two types, giving everyone some high-priced wine to sell. In the past, the *Companhia* simply indicated *tonel* by *tonel* which market the wine inside qualified for.[49] It had long been accused of inconsistency and capriciousness, but there was no logical objection to the claim that the contents of one *tonel* were better than another. This year, defying all logic, it regularly split *toneis* in two, so that a single lot of wine comprised two qualities, half deemed suitable for the British market and half not, though the wine inside was identical.[50]

The *Companhia* also permitted exporters to Britain to buy the *séparado* wine. British firms initially bought only the *legal* as, trading only to Britain, they had no use for the other wine. Farmers with exceptionally good wine, however, learned to refuse to sell their *legal* if purchasers would not buy the *separado* too. This perplexed the British, few of whom traded in the *separado* markets. But the *Companhia* then took two more steps that dealt both with this problem and with the stocks of inferior wine that had accumulated in Oporto from the previous poor harvests.

Wine had to travel with *bilhetes*. These were certificates that identified the quality of the wine. The *Companhia* now legitimised the (de facto well-established) trade in *bilhetes*. A merchant with poor *legal* wine of previous vintages could now sell the wine but retain the certificate permitting export to Britain. He could also buy superior wine that, having been classed as *separado* this year, lacked such certification (and so sold at a cheaper price). Thus, holders of the qualified but poor *legal* of 1817, 1818, and 1819 could now trade it for the good but unqualified *separado* of 1820. Those who ended up with the poor wine could send it to the *separado* market, while those with the good wine could send it to the British market, although it had not originally been qualified or priced for this.[51]

This ruling quickly led to a good deal of wine swapping as the British sought to empty their lodges of poor wine. An elaborate market in *bilhetes* developed, pushing good quality wine towards the high-quality and high-priced British market while drawing the lower quality wines towards the lower-priced markets. Those who began the year with low quality *legal* ended the year with high quality *legal* without being forced to dump their prior holdings at a loss. The *Companhia's* actions thus helped to shore up the largest stockholders, who had most to lose from rapid depreciation.[52]

This action also helped to segment the market. For the question that remained, of course, was what would happen to all this *separado*? In the following year, the *Companhia's* tight hold on the Brazil market was loosened and Latin America quickly became the major market for private shippers who as a result of the swap had acquired large quantities of wine not qualified for the British market. From 1,200 pipes in 1821, Latin American imports of *separado* leapt to 10,270 by 1825. The decision not only separated the wine, it also separated the shippers. British firms in Oporto had little interest and less experience in the *separado* market in general and in South America in particular. Consequently, wine unsuitable for the British market quickly flowed over to those who could sell it in Brazil, and these were primarily Portuguese. Only one of the top ten exporters in the *separado* trade was British. In exchange, the Portuguese merchants could pass their *legal* wine to exporters to the British market, where they were generally less adept. For this to work, the *Companhia* seems to have relaxed its formerly aggressive stance towards Portuguese merchants acting as brokers between farmers and exporters, and a lucrative internal market in wine for Britain developed.[53]

Dividing the British

The *Companhia's* combined actions, as ever seeking to rule by division, undoubtedly served the British well in a time of crisis. In particular, it allowed the British to find an outlet for the poor quality wine from the three previous poor harvests. In so doing, it gave merchants the resources to clear their old debts and buy the wine of the excellent harvests of 1820 and 1821. Gassiot, a partner in Martinez, reported that the rule of thumb for port shippers was, 'If it is a fine vintage, sell your shirt to buy wine', and these two years were very fine vintages. The new rules, however, allowed exporters to sell their old stocks rather than their shirts.[54]

So the *Companhia's* actions divided the British from the Portuguese, pushing one community towards the British market and the other towards the Latin American. In part as a consequence of this action, the British, led by firms in our group, began a steady climb back to dominance in the 1820s, as Table 2 indicated. Table 4 shows the fruit of that progress, giving their position in the new, free market era after the *Companhia's* abolition. The British collectively then accounted for almost half the exporters to Britain as well as two-thirds of the trade, portions they had not held for fifty years. And the top firm, Sandeman provided ten per cent of exports, a portion no private house had aspired to since Offley in 1792.

Table 4: Ranking in list of exporters compared to other British firms and to all firms, with per cent market share (by volume)[55]

Rank	1837–40		
	British	All	% total
Taylor	11	13	2
Croft	9	11	3
Hunt	7	9	3
Offley	6	8	3
Swann	n/a	n/a	n/a
Martinez	10	12	3
Sandeman	1	1	10
Cockburn	18	23	1
Number of equivalent firms (1/H)[56]		16	
Average number of exporters	27	56	

n/a= not applicable

How much did the *Companhia* contribute to this new British dominance? Helping restore the British firms to financial health made one contribution. Segmenting the trade and thus excluding Portuguese competition made another. In 1820, the British controlled only 46 per cent of exports. By 1832, before the Civil War cut off trade, the figure had risen to 65 per cent – a dominance they carried over into the free-market era. By 1840, there were only three Portuguese firms in the top twenty exporters.

But the *Companhia's* actions also served to divide the British community internally. They seem to have been designed to shore up the conventional firms and their conventional strategies by allowing them to regain stability through the curious separation of the wine. But that was not the only effect the new regulations had. For among the firms in our group, a new division is visible. In the period under discussion, the old guard, though still a force in the trade, give way to the new. By 1832, Sandeman, established in Oporto for barely 15 years, had become the leading British exporter, toppling Offley, who had held the position as if by right for most of seven decades. By 1837, Martinez, only back in the trade for three years was in second place, pushing aside firms that among them had more than 300 years' experience. While by 1841 Cockburn, a parvenu from 1815, was established in the top ten. These are not serendipitous results. In the second half of the century, these three firms are regularly the top three exporters (with another new entrant, Grahams, which arrived in 1826, regularly in fourth).

So the question then remains, is there anything distinctive about the behaviour of these three firms? Were old strategies giving way to new, or just old firms? The most obvious distinction, the biggest shift in strategy is evident in their use of debt. As we noted, the old firms were almost constitutionally afraid of debt and followed a conservative route, financing investment in wine primarily out of capital. The new firms turned out to be less cautious. And their boldness was, we believe, unintentionally supported by the *Companhia's* action.

Table 5: Working capital (*mil reis*)

	1812–20	1821–34	1835–40
Campbell	103,560	[-]	n/a
Croft	123,961	136,249	[-]
Hunt	300,218	193,335	131,291
Offley	66,064	279,130	257,878
Swann	238,149	[-]	n/a
Martinez	[-]	–52,063	–66,237
Sandeman	37,771	–41,278	–265,177
Cockburn	25,999	–725	78,407

n/a= not applicable; [-] = not available

In an attempt to reveal the changing use of debt, Table 5 shows the firms' 'working capital' according to available balance sheets.[59] This was the money ideally available to them if they were forced to liquidate their stock and settle their debts. Thus it includes their various assets (cash, wine, casks, and accounts receivable) less their accounts payable. The lower the figure, the more indebted and the more at risk a particular firm is. A negative figure suggests that the firm's wine (which was its principal asset) was funded on debt. A negative or low sum in this business was particularly risky, because, as we have suggested, wine stocks could depreciate very rapidly in face of a slump in the trade or a bountiful harvest.

In the hard times of the post-war period, the old firms were generally conservative in their use of debt. Offley is an exception. For such a large firm, it let its working capital sink quite low as it struggled to regain dominance. It got away with this – others in the sector, as we have seen, were not so lucky and fell insolvent. The new firms in our group, Cockburn and Sandeman, also have lower figures, but this is because as newcomers they had tighter budgets with less padding. In the *Companhia*-aided recovery of the 1820s, however, the distinction between old and new is sharper. Offley and Croft, averse as we argued to risk, took advantage of the return of solid profitability to climb away from debt, funding their business out of their growing capital accounts. Hunt's accounts do move in the opposite direction, but its lower figure primarily reflects the firm's retreat from the wine trade. It had little or no wine to contribute to the positive side of its working capital. In fact, its credit balance (primarily bills and accounts receivable, but also large amounts of cash) was so high for the period 1820–30 that the firm actually earned more in interest than from wine.[60]

In the later periods, the new firms make a marked contrast. All have negative balances at some point. Cockburn climbs back into the positive in the post-Civil War period, but given the increasing size of its business, its working capital remains remarkably low. All three, these figures suggest, and certainly Sandeman and Martinez, took advantage of the recovery to dig themselves further into debt. Martinez's reincarnation traded only in the free-trade era. But Sandeman having learned to live with risk under the *Companhia's* tutelage traded much more aggressively than its older rivals. In 1821, wine provided 98 per cent of its collateral, leaving very little room for manoeuvre if prices fell – and between 1819 and 1820 the value of wine held in this group had fallen 20 per cent, so the risk was very real. The house was in effect kept afloat through the *Companhia's* good graces as its regulations provided an outlet for the depreciating old wine. But, with that help, the risk was rewarded. Sandeman's wine account in 1821 made more money than it had for the years 1816 to 1820 combined. And in 1822, with another excellent harvest available, it was able to spend more on wine than it ever had before.

Having learned such risk taking under the *Companhia*, the new firms continued to live with debt, relying increasingly on the credit of their suppliers. In so doing, they drew Portuguese capital into that part of the export trade from which it had been implicitly denied direct access by the *Companhia's* divide and rule policy. In the late 1820s, for example, Sandeman's debt to Portuguese suppliers began to rise. The firm began to rely not just on the small farmers of the Douro, but on large landholders and city merchants. These would supply wine on credit. Then at the height of the war, when the bar of Oporto had been closed and no one had any income, Sandeman made unprecedented purchases of almost 8,000 pipes of wine, all paid for with long-term credit, from the Ferreira family, the most substantial winegrower in the Douro and one of Oporto's wealthiest merchants.

This was a firm of Portuguese farmers and merchants that had tried to establish an agency in Britain and compete in the export trade after the Napoleonic wars.[61] In the 1820s, however, it had followed the lines laid down by the *Companhia's* division of the trade, retreating from exports and expanding its vineyards in the Douro and brokering wine between farmers and British export houses. Ferreira debt and Ferreira wine helped propel Sandeman to the dominant position it held after the Civil War, for when trade with Britain reopened, Sandeman had sufficient wine to meet the unslaked thirst of the British market. It was to the Ferreiras, too, that Jones, the Oporto resident of Martinez, turned for credit when he reestablished the business in 1834.[62] Again, with Ferreira wine and Ferreira loans, Martinez quickly rose to stand immediately behind Sandeman in the list of exporters.

It seems reasonable to argue, therefore, that the risk that, in the 1820s, was encouraged by the *Companhia*, was, after its collapse, underwritten by those Portuguese who, guided by *Companhia* promptings, had turned from the export trade to Britain and instead cultivated their vineyards and the internal market. If this is the case, then, intriguingly, the triumphant emergence of the firms in the free-market era may be traced, not simply to the institutions of that market alone and the adventurous policies of the British entrepreneurs working under minimal restraint, but along a path of strategies and actions whose initial success depended on mercantile regulation, the policy of divide and rule, and merchants' reaction to that policy.

CONCLUSION

We have looked in some detail at the activities of a group of British merchant houses established, or in some cases, reestablished overseas in the years following the Napoleonic wars. This period was one of remarkable transformation for British merchant enterprise in general. Many of the props on which traders had come directly or indirectly to rely were swept away, as a changed economic and political world emerged in the post-war years. Among these disappearing props in the port trade, which provides a useful window onto the agents of change in the merchants' world more generally, were regulation and conservative financial practices. Regulation had long played a critical role in shaping the port trade. It had restricted (or at least, restricted the need for) backward integration, both from London to Oporto and from Oporto to the Douro where the wine was grown. Instead the regulation had implicitly favoured a group of independently financed partnerships trading principally on British capital.

As that capital dried up in the post-war years, however, both regulation and financial strategies changed. The regulators, acting to protect the diminishing capital of the firms, further segmented the market dividing the British from the Portuguese. In the wake of these actions, we have argued, it is possible to see a further division, this time among the strategies of the firms. Members of what we have called the 'old guard', historically averse to debt, used the regulator's added protection to return to their old capital- and profit-hoarding strategies. Newer firms, less influenced by the role of capital in the history of the trade, took advantage of regulatory support to move in exactly the opposite direction. They took greater risks, buying wine not with capital, but with debt. Thus the new British firms benefited not only from the absence of Portuguese competitors (as the old guard did), but also from the availability of Portuguese capital which they drew back into the trade in the form of long-term bills used to purchase wine. As the new firms rose on the back of these practices to dominate the trade in the free-market era, it seems reasonable to conclude that the shape of the market in that era was significantly determined by the prior actions we have been describing. Thus, though formal institutional controls were abolished with the end of Portuguese absolutism in 1834, their influence can be traced in the shape of the trade and its finances in the subsequent free-market era. Markets as well as firms, this argument suggests, are open to evolutionary explanation.

NOTES

* Research for this article was conducted with the generous support of the National Endowment for the Humanities, Collaborative Projects Division; and the Fundação Luso-Americana para o Desenvolvimento both directly and through the intervention of the Portuguese Studies Program at UC Berkeley. It also relies on the generosity of private and public institutions that hold records of the port trade. We would like to acknowledge the generous help of the following (names are followed by the abbreviations used in the notes): A. A. Ferreira, records of the Ferreira family and Hunt, Newman, Roope (AAF); Offley Forrester (OFW); The House of Sandeman,

records of Sandeman & Co (S&Co); Cockburn Smithes, records of Cockburn, Wauchope, Greig and Martinez, Jones, Gassiot (CS); Taylor, Fladgate Yeatman, records of Campbell, Bowden, Taylor, John Taylor, Sobral & Pinto (CBT); Croft & Co (Croft); Public Record Office (PRO); University of California, Davis, Special Collections (UCD); Real Companhia Velha, records of Companhia Geral das Vinhas do Alto Douro (RCV); Guildhall Library (GLD), Torre do Tombo (TdoT).

We would like to thank Terry Gourvish for insightful comments.

1. For such discussions, see for example, special issues of *Business History*, 1997, 34 (9) and *Scandinavian Economic History Review*, 1999, 47 (1).
2. For details of the regulation, see the account of the *Companhia Geral da Agricultura das Vinhas do Alto Douro*, below.
3. For a study of contemporary demarcation in the context of regulation theory, see G. Haughton & J. Browett, 'Flexible Theory and Flexible Regulation: Collaboration and Competition in the Mclaren Vale Wine Industry in South Australia' *Environment & Planning*, 1995, 27 (1), pp. 41–62. We will not be dealing with formal regulation theory in this paper.
4. For the political outlook of merchants in this period see Stanley Chapman, *Merchant Enterprise in Britain: From the Industrial Revolution to World War I* (Cambridge, 1992); David Hancock, *Citizens of the World: London Merchants and the Integration of the British Atlantic Economy* (New York, 1995).
5. For accounts based on these sources, see A.D. Francis, *The Wine Trade* (London, 1972); L.M.E. Shaw, *The Anglo-Portuguese Alliance and the English Merchants in Portugal, 1654–1810* (Aldershot, 1998).
6. James Warre, *The Past, Present & Probably the Future State of the Wine Trade: Proving that an Increase of Duty Caused a Decrease of Revenue* (London, 1823); Fleetwood Williams, *Observations on the State of the Wine Trade, Occasioned by the Perusal of a Pamphlet on the Same Subject by Mr. Warre* (London, 1824). See also 'A Portuguese', *The Wine Question Considered: or Observations on the Pamphlets of Mr James Warre & Mr Fleetwood Williams Respecting the General Company for the Agriculture of the Vineyards of the Upper Douro* (London, 1824).
7. UCD, 'Madeira Merchants' (D16). Thomas Gordon, London, to Newton, Gordon, & Murdoch, Funchal, Madeira, 3 July 1794.
8. Sandeman & Co, Porto to Sandeman, Gooden & Forster, London, 24 July 1821.
9. Ronald H. Coase, 'The Firm, the Market, & the Law': 1–31 in idem, *The Firm, the Market, & the Law* (Chicago, 1988), p. 9.
10. For a recent account that assumes the merchants' protests were an open reflection of their interests and so that the merchants themselves were (and should have been) simply opposed to the port regulations, see Shaw, *The Anglo-Portuguese*.
11. For a similar argument, see John Vincent Nye, 'The Myth of Free-Trade Britain and Fortress France: Tariffs and Trade in the Nineteenth Century,' *Journal of Economic History*, 1991, 51 (1), pp. 23–46.
12. Chapman, *Merchants*.

13. For details of the British Factories in Portugal and their operation, see John Delaforce, *The Factory House at Oporto* (Bromley, 1990); H.V. Livermore, 'The Privileges of an Englishman in the Kingdoms and Dominions of Portugal,' *Atlante*, 1954, 2 (2), pp. 59–77.

14. With few exceptions, British exporters bought the wine that they exported. They neither grew grapes nor made wine. This was done by Portuguese.

15. For history of this trade and its treaties, see V.M. Shillington and A.B. Wallis Chapman, *The Commercial Relations of England and Portugal* (London, 1903). Francisco Ribeiro da Silva, 'Do Douro ao Porto: O Protagonismo do Vinho na Época Moderna', *Douro: Estudos e Documentos*, 1996, 1 (2): 93–118. Conceição Andrade Martins, 'Vinha, Vinho e Política Vinícola em Portugal: Do Pombalismo à Regeneração', 3 vols. Dissertação de Doutoramento, Universidade de Évora (Portugal, 1999); Susan Cora Schneider, *O Marquês de Pombal*, J. Oliveira Marques (trans.) (Lisbon, 1980); Jorge Borges de Macedo, *A Situação Económica no Tempo de Pombal: Alguns Aspectos*, 3rd ed. (Lisbon, 1989).

16. There were two more principal categories: *ramo*, or tavern wine and *refugado*, wine fit only for distillation.

17. Along with British merchants, some exporters from Northern Europe also established houses in Oporto. See our mention of the Dutch family, VanZellers, below.

18. *Instituição da Companhia Geral da Agricultura das Vinhas do Alto Douro* (Lisbon, 1756); Álvaro Moreira da Fonseca, *As Demarcações Pombalinas no Douro Vinhateiro*, 3 vols. (Oporto, 1949–51). António M. de Barros Cardoso, 'O Alvará de Instituição da Companhia e os Motins do Porto de 1757', *Douro: Estudos e Documentos*, 1996, 1 (1). pp. 57–78.

19. 'Since the decease of the late King', Sir John Croft wrote in 1788, 'though the Wine Company still subsists, there is a greater latitude shewn by them to the English, in respect to their purchasing of wines ... and a much greater allowance and indulgence from the Portuguese Wine Company in respect to a free trade'. John Croft, *A Treatise on the Wines of Portugal*. (London, 1788), p. 13. For the changes in the Companhia, see also Gaspar Martins Pereira, *O Douro e o Vinho do Porto: De Pombal a João Franco* (Oporto, 1991).

20. Consul Whitehead's response to a Board of Trade questionnaire on the state of the trade, in 1786, PRO, BT 6 63.

21. Norman R. Bennett, 'The Golden Age of the Port Wine System, 1781–1807', *International History Review*, 1990, 12 (2), pp. 221–248.

22. Export share is by volume. As the *Companhia*, the main Portuguese competitor of the British merchants, competed by undercutting their prices, the British share of the market by value is probably higher. Data on exports for 1777, 1786, 1796, and 1805 come from Arquivo do Torre de Tombo: Alfândega [Customs House] do Porto, Mesa do Consulado e Fragatas, Saídas (127, 277, 444, 770, and 1046). Export data for British firms, 1792 to 1810, from T.G. Shaw, *Wine, the Vine, and the Cellar*, 2d ed. (London, 1864). Exporters and exported volumes for 1809–32 from the annual lists published by the Alfândega do Porto; for 1837 and later from the *Folha Mercantil*

do Porto. Total export volumes from Conceição Andrade Martins, *Memória do Vinho do Porto* (Lisbon, 1990), quad 66.

23. Of the firms we discuss, Hunt had an informal agreement to buy the wine of the Oratório (a monastery in the city of Oporto with extensive farms in the Douro) each year. See Gaspar Martins Pereira, 'As Quintas do Oratório do Porto no Alto Douro', *Revista de História Económica e Social*, 1984, 13, pp. 13–50.

24. In the post-Civil War era, Offley both leased the Quinta de Boa Vista and entered long-term contracts for wine from the Ferreira family, whom we discuss briefly below.

25. Chapman, *Merchant Enterprise*: xiv. Jorge Borges de Macedo, *O Bloqueio Continental* (Lisbon, 1990). Paul Duguid, 'The Changing of the Guard: British Firms in the Port Trade (1777–1849)', in G.M. Pereira (ed.), *O Vinho do Porto no Século XIX*, (forthcoming).

26. In 1838, the government established a much weaker regulatory body, with few of the powers that made its predecessor so powerful. This limped along until 1865, when it and the demarcation were abolished.

27. Martinez appears to have made two attempts to gain a foothold, the first during the war, perhaps in 1809, the second after, in 1834.

28. Regarding it as a distinct entity, we do not consider the firm of Taylor in our discussion of Campbell.

29. In what follows, we call the firms in Table 1 by the name of their first partner, e.g. "Campbell". Dates on the origins of the pre-Pombaline companies come from Charles Sellers, *Oporto Old and New* (Oporto, 1899, privately printed). Swann's comes from Alfândega data as in note 22. The newcomers' dates come from the firm's surviving records, except for the first Martinez date, which comes again from the Alfândega records and the *Registos dos Privilégios* livro 14, in the Arquivo Distrital do Porto. Financial data come from the firms' records. Data for Swann come from surviving records of Sobral & Pinto, the firm's procurement arm from 1816–19. For the relations of all these firms to houses in Britain, see Paul Duguid and Teresa Silva Lopes, 'Ambiguous Company: Institutions and Organizations in the Port Wine Trade, 1814–1834', *Scandinavian Economic History Review*, 1999, 47 (1), pp. 84–103.

30. Volume is measured in pipes or *pipas*, a barrel holding approximately 550 litres. The Companhia ranked first among exporters in every year from 1812 to 1830. Export lists suggest Swann Knowsley ceased trading in 1830.

31. The British firm of Butler & Tyndale ranked above Offley in 1812. In later years, this firm allied itself closely to Portuguese houses so it seems reasonable to suspect that it did so in this year, too.

32. Price data from Martins, *Memória* quad. 36.

33. AAF, T.H. Hunt, Maisonette to Hunt (Oporto), 25 October 1815.

34. Larry Neal, 'The Finance of Business during the Industrial Revolution', in Roderick Floud and Donald McCloskey (eds.), *The Economic History of Britain since 1700* Vol. 1, 2nd ed. (Cambridge, 1994).

35. Hancock, *Citizens of the World*, p. 411, shows the sugar traders of the period averaging between 8 and 10 per cent, with lows of 3.5 and highs of

13.5 per cent. For the difficulty of understanding profit historically, see also Richard Grassby, 'The Rate of Profit in Seventeenth-Century England', *English Historical Review* 1969, 84 (October), pp. 721–751; G.A. Lee, 'The Concept of Profit in British Accounting, 1760–1900'. *Business History Review*, 1975, 49 (1), pp. 6–36.

36. Hunt did not distribute the dividends for the 1812–20 period until 1829.

37. The nominal exchange rate of the period was 64d to the mil reis (so there were just under 4 mil reis to the pound sterling), though the actual rate fluctuated wildly. Cockburn's figures are for the years 1815–17 and 1825 only. Swann's for 1816–18. Martinez's for 1834 only. Hunt's accounting periods ran from July 1809 to December 1812 and from January 1813 to March 1820.

38. As the century advanced, the taste for older wines increased, thus the port trade went against the general trend, described by Chapman, of reduced stock holding. This again must have made it hard for the port trade to attract capital away from other businesses (Chapman, *Merchants*, 196ff.)

39. AAF, Hunt, Newman, Roope, Porto, to TH Hunt, Maisonette, 25 October 1815, and below.

40. See Hancock, *Citizens*, p. 247 on the general preference for capital rather than debt.

41. AAF, T.H. Hunt, Maisonette, to Hunt, Porto, 25 October 1815.

42. S&Co, Sandeman to Robert H. Clarke, London, 9 September 1820.

43. See James Warre, *Past, Present* for Warre's claim to be a general trader.

44. See Table 5, below.

45. Croft, *Treatise*.

46. See, for example, Anon., *Considerações Fundadas em Factos sobre a Extinção da Companhia do Porto* (Rio de Janeiro, 1812); J. da Silva, *Memória Economica Sobre a Franqueza do Commercio dos Vinhos do Porto* (Rio de Janeiro, 1812); Anon. *Original Documents Respecting the Injurious Effects and the Impolicy of a Further Continuation of the Portuguese Royal Wine Company of Oporto* (London, 1813); [Correspondentes da Companhia Geral], *Relação dos Factos Praticados pela Commissão dos Commerciantes de Vinhos, em Londres, Correspondentes da Companhia Geral: Em consequencia da Petição appresentada á Camara dos Communs em 12 de Julho . . . por certas pessoas, que se intitulão Membros da Extincta Feitora* (Lisbon, 1813).

47. A.D. Francis suggests that Portuguese exporters of this period were merely fronts for British houses, thus their disappearance would be a simple result of the British return. Many of these firms, however, though undoubtedly benefiting from the blockade, were in the export trade well before, and had continued in business after the British returned. See A.D. Francis, *Wine Trade* and Duguid, 'Changing of the Guard'.

48. The northern European market was inconsequential.

49. Wine was kept in a *tonel* (plural *toneis*) or large, immobile vat that contained about thirteen pipes. The wine was transferred to pipes for transport.

50. The *Companhia* had previously tried to redistribute the purchase to favour smaller farmers, which was the effective outcome of the strategy of 1821. See, for example, the *Edital* (or edict) of 18 October 1776. In 1821, when

accused of being slow in organising the wine purchases that year, the *Companhia* defended itself by lamenting that the new qualification, in which almost every farmer now had two types of wine, required its deputies to fill out twice as many forms. See the *Junta da Administração* of the *Companhia's* reply to its critics, written by Antonio Thomas d'Almeida da Silva [UCD, D-283, ms sources III].

51. For the Portuguese trade in *bilhetes* (or *guias*), see Gaspar Martins Pereira and Maria Luísa Nicolau de Almeida de Olazabal, *Dona Antónia* (Oporto, 1996) p. 24.

52. For one of the fullest accounts of this procedure, which carefully prices the *bilhetes*, see the anonymous pamphlet, *Memória Sobre o Direito que Assiste aos Negociantes de Vinhos do Douro para Reclamar do Governo de SMF a Indemnização dos Prejuízos que lhes Cauzo o Decreto de 30 de Maio de 1834* (Oporto, 1840).

53. For a discussion of Portuguese difficulties in the British market, see Paul Duguid, 'Institutional Asymmetries: Economics and Culture in the Development of the Port Wine Market', paper presented at the Symposion de la Asociación Internacional de Historia y Civilización de la Vid y el Vino. El Puerto de Santa María, Spain, 18–20 March 1999. For the brokers, see Paul Duguid, 'Lavradores, Exportadores'.

54. Gassiot quoted in Shaw, *Wine*, p. 176.

55. These data, unlike those in Table 2, are taken from the *Folha Mercantil*. This only listed firms exporting more than 100 pipes, thus the actual share of the total of each firm would actually be slightly lower, and the number of exporters slightly higher. As Sandeman exported a good deal of wine that did not make the lists in this period, its listed portion may actually understate its true share. See Paul Duguid, 'Speculations on "Change"', paper presented at the conference 'The Anglo-Portuguese Alliance in History, 1373–1993: Reappraisals', Cambridge, UK, 20–24 September 1993.

56. See Table 2.

57. Portuguese capital, however, was involved in the British trade, as many British were dependent on it. See Duguid and Silva Lopes, 'Ambiguous Company'.

58. We will not know the *Companhid's* intentions until the archive of its deliberations is open to researchers.

59. Cockburn's balance sheets were only available for 1815, 1825, 1835, and 1840. Martinez for 1834 and 1835. Before 1832, Sandeman only balanced accounts sporadically, so its figures reflect our extrapolation. Lacunae in accounts inevitably makes some of the argument presented here speculative.

60. It may only be coincidence that by the end of the period, two of the three that avoided debt in the first years, Campbell and Swann, had gone out of business.

61. For Ferreira's attempts to enter the export trade, see Gonçalves Guimarães, *Um Português em Londres* (A.A. Ferreira SA, Arquivo Histórico, 1988).

62. Hunt, intriguingly, provided Cockburn's initial credit.

Business Education in Britain and Italy: a Long Term Perspective (1860s–1940s)*

Francesca Fauri

University of Bologna

This paper examines the various efforts to launch business education in Britain and Italy, and evaluates the relative successes and failures of business studies in the two countries. Britain and Italy represent an interesting comparative case. They have shown a similar development pattern from an accounting approach into an organisational one and they have been struck approximately at the same time by the impact of the American management doctrine (see Table 1). The analysis will shed some light on the two different economic and cultural reactions to the American impact. To a certain extent, Italian economic backwardness led to greater government interest in support for technical and management education, whereas Britain's leading position in the industrial revolution reinforced the view of most businessmen and industrialists that learning on the job, as they had always done, was the best way for the next generation to prepare, albeit with some significant exceptions.

The British case is discussed in the light of two opposite interpretations. Some authors (Locke, Rose, Sanderson, Wiener) believe that the preference of British industrialists for classical education proved wholly inadequate in preparing their sons as future industrial managers. In the words of Locke, Britain was missing the technical educational complement essential to modern entrepreneurial activity. Others (Church, Rubinstein, Wilson) support instead the thesis that British economic performance and decline in industrial spirit of third generation owners was not different from her rivals and that the influence of family capitalism versus trained management was a common feature of many countries.[1]

In the Italian case the debate, even though more limited in scope, has pointed to an overemphasis of classical education producing a plethora of unemployed or in the words of Barbagli, 'educating for unemployment'.[2] However, this hides the existence in certain areas of the country of a good supply of technical education.[3] The fascist school reform of 1923 (*Riforma*

Table 1: Most important institutions and courses influencing the
development of business studies at a higher level

Italy	Great Britain
Turin Polytechnic (1860) Industrial engineering specialisation 1928 Management courses	*Birmingham Faculty of Commerce* *(1899)* Business oriented commerce courses
Milan Polytechnic (1863) Industrial engineering specialisation 1875 Course on industrial economics 1928 Management courses 1935 Post-graduate school of business	*Regent Street Polytechnic (1881)* 1919–20 Management courses 1925 Department of business administration
	Institute of Industrial Administration *(1919)*
Genoa High School of Commerce *(1884)* 1919 One year specialisation in industrial economics and administration	*Manchester College (1899)* 1926 Post graduate business school
Bocconi High School of Commerce *(1902)* 1920 Laboratory for business studies	*London School of Economics and* *Political Sciences (1902)* 1902 Business oriented accounting courses 1930 Post graduate business school
Venice High School of Commerce *(1868)* 1934 Post-graduate course in business administration	

Gentile), replacing Technical Schools with complementary institutes with
no further educational outlets and limiting university access to the students coming out from the *licei* (classical schools), caused an immediate
fall in engineering and High School of Commerce registrations.[4] The effects on Italian technical education were deleterious, technical schools
diplomas lost status and were deprived of their traditional outlet, the
polytechnics, causing a sharp fall in student enrolments (from 11,307
students enrolled in 1921 the number drops to 4,106 in 1931). Nonetheless, attention to business education continued to develope despite the
classical rhetoric of the fascist regime and its efforts aimed at instituting a
corporate form of economic system.

Finally, this paper also aims at throwing light on the fact that, despite
the current entrepreneurs' assertion that 'managers are born not made', in

both countries the forces materially financing many management training courses belong to the business community.

TECHNICAL SECONDARY SCHOOLS

Some authors have suggested the existence of a strict link between entrepreneurial performance and education and, in more recent times, higher education.[5] According to Locke for instance, higher education can be held partially responsible for the ensuing disappointing or successful economic results in a country's long term history. From a general historical perspective, the development pattern of higher education in Britain and Italy ran on very dissimilar tracks. Italy was characterised by public education and in particular by a great emphasis on technical education, whereas British education was largely private and with a strong anti-science bias. In Italy, two years before unification, the *Legge Casati* was passed (1859), modernising and innovating Italy's educational system. The Casati Act covered all levels and branches of education and laid down the general outlines of the new system. Not only was elementary education made free and compulsory for four years (ten years before a similar step was taken in Britain with the 1870 Education Act), but secondary education was diversified into three types: classical, technical and teachers' training schools.[6] The real novelty of the Casati Act was the introduction of a new, scientifically oriented course of study of technical instruction at the lower, intermediate and university level. On the eve of unification, free commercial and technical secondary schools were established in several parts of Italy. Furthermore, other technical institutes of a more vocational character were set up by local entrepreneurial and financial forces. Their syllabi were not rigid and the schools were supervised by the Ministry of Agriculture, Industry and Commerce. Classes were often held in the evening and this was the main difference with the technical schools.[7] The greatest increase was that experienced by the *Scuole d'arti e mestieri,* which attracted 0.8 per cent of secondary school students in 1862 and 18 per cent in 1915. One of the most famous and interesting examples, important for its shaping of the intellectual and industrial elite in Milan, was the Society for the Encouragement of Art and Industry (SIAM) founded by Enrico Mylius in 1839 with the support of the industrial-mercantile upper-middle class. Teachers included personalities such as Giovanni Cantoni, Giovanni Battista Pirelli, Giuseppe Colombo and Gabrio Casati, later to be found among the founders of the Milan Polytechnic.[8] Technical education spread quickly: the number of students attending lower and intermediate technical schools increased from 27 per cent of the total in 1862 to 35 per cent in 1915 and reached 60 per cent after the Second World War.[9] Technical education took off at the end of the nineteenth century, and it was not just the number of students that changed, since the social composition of the students enrolled shifted towards higher standards. The class difference between grammar and technical schools gradually weakened.

In the British case, among the many reasons why the advance of technical instruction was held back was the English attitude to education. The concept of a liberal education lay at the very root of an English educational philosophy firmly based on the study of classics and mathematics.[10] It was very difficult for newer scientific disciplines, as well as for technical schools, to establish themselves and become popular. Numerous state acts (1889 Technical Instruction Act, 1890 Local Taxation Act and 1902 Education Act) encouraged the expansion of technical education, but with limited success in terms of number of students. In particular, the 1889 Technical Instruction Act originated from the 'traumatic experience of the 1867 Paris Exhibition', which established the fact that some foreign countries were making greater progress in manufacturing industry than Great Britain itself, thus increasing the fears of British weaknesses and retardation of growth.[11] The ensuing Royal Commissions' inquiries into the provision for technical education in the country led to the 1889 Act, which permitted local authorities to levy rates to aid technical or manual instruction.[12] Additional financial aid was provided by the Local Taxation (Customs and Excise) Act of 1890, which diverted 'whisky money' to local authorities to assist technical education or relieve rates. As one MP ironically observed, this 'whisky money' enabled local authorities 'to distil wisdom out of whisky, genius out of gin and capacity for business out of beer'.[13] The injection of 'whisky money' was timely and life-saving for a number of institutions later to become technical colleges.

With the passing of the Education Act 1902 and the promulgation of Regulations for Junior Technical Schools in 1913, further encouragement was given to the expansion of technical education.[14] Junior Technical Schools were fee paying schools, often more expensive than grammar schools. The 13 year age of entry was set with the assumption that they should lead immediately to work and not to further study. University access was thus not formally but practically restrained to the students of grammar schools. Junior Technical Schools' former pupils went directly into productive industrial careers and sometimes reached managerial positions rising from a technical base. Only 20 new technical schools were built between 1902 and 1918, giving a total of 31 local technical schools with 2,768 students. After the 1944 Education Act, technical schools declined and were swallowed up into grammar and comprehensive schools. Technical schools always attracted a very small number of students (1.4 per cent in the interwar years) and were constantly eclipsed by the more popular grammar and public schools. Young graduates from technical institutes rarely entered university (even though their preparation was sometimes of university standard), they undertook careers in industry with no further formal training and in not just a few cases were able to reach managerial positions.[15]

Among the various British examples, the story of the Regent Street Polytechnic (recently developed into the University of Westminster) is of particular interest, since it was one of the first institutes to offer management courses in its engineering and commercial schools.[16] As was recognised by contemporary observers, a lot of work done at the Polytechnic in the last quarter of the nineteenth century was of distinctly university standard. A considerable number of students aspired to a university degree and presented themselves every half-year for the London matriculation examination: many were able to pass it with the preparation obtained from the ordinary classes at the Polytechnic.

By the end of the century nearly every other London polytechnic found itself compelled to make express provision for students who were working for university degrees. This development of an 'evening class university' was one of the most remarkable educational advances made in London at the time.[17] At the engineering day school of the Regent Street Polytechnic the work done by the second and third year students in the classes and laboratories practically covered the syllabuses for the University of London degree in engineering and for the examinations of the Institution of Civil Engineers.[18] After the First World War, the Polytechnic was among the first institutions to introduce courses on management education. In the 1919–20 session, the school of engineering was enriched by two new courses on management introduced in the fourth year: elements of engineering management and economics of engineering management.[19] Three years later, in 1922, at the School of Commerce and Business Training, a new course was set up: industrial management taught by J. Lee, who had just published a book on management and on the need to recognise managers as 'an expert professional class'.[20] Finally, in 1925, a department of industrial administration was founded to teach, among others, courses on business practice and statistics, costing and cost accounts and works organisation and management.[21] As specified in the syllabus, the department was established to meet a new but rapidly growing need in technical education:

> The changes in the structure of industry have brought with them new demands on the management. In the past men could grow up in a business and gain sufficiently wide experience to qualify him to manage such a concern efficiently. Possessing the right personality a man could gain sufficient knowledge to make him an efficient manager. Today the conditions have changed. The typical business unit is larger ... business relations have become more complex ... state regulation and restrictions increase almost daily. Under these circumstances new methods of training in the embryo administrator must be sought.[22]

Soon after, Elbourne (the founder of the Institute of Industrial Administration in 1919) joined Adams as head of the department conferring from 1928 his engineering imprint to the four year course. The department aimed at providing 'co-ordinated instruction and training for those intending to qualify for responsible administrative positions in industry'. After the Second World War, a department on management studies was founded, providing courses to attain the intermediate certificate in management studies (a one year day course or a three year evening course) awarded by the British Institute of Management and the Ministry of Education.[24]

One difference that can be highlighted is that if in Italy the bulk of engineering and commerce faculties' students were technical schools graduates (at least until the 1923 Gentile reform) in Britain access to university was severely limited for technical schools students. Yet, technical colleges' preparation was valuable and often innovative, as the example of the management courses offered inside the Regent Street Polytechnic has shown.

THE MANAGEMENT EDUCATION OF ENGINEERS

In Italy, thanks to the Casati Act, university education was enriched with high technical schools (polytechnics), two of which were opened almost immediately in Milan and Turin. Access to the polytechnics was initially limited to students having successfully attended the first two years of the faculty of mathematics and physics. Milan and Turin remained the leading centres for engineering education in Italy until the First World War and were the first schools to offer degrees in industrial as well as civil engineering. In 1870, 82 civil and three industrial engineers graduated from the Turin Polytechnic, while 61 civil and nine industrial engineers achieved a degree from Milan. By 1880, attendance in these sections began to increase rapidly, signifying a growing confidence in the new degree, and by the end of the century, enrolments in industrial engineering outnumbered those in civil engineering. In 1912, 23 civil and 98 industrial engineers graduated in Milan and 53 civil and 125 industrial in Turin.[24]

The close relationship between the school and the entrepreneurial community can be illustrated by the occupational status of the engineers graduating from the Milan Polytechnic. Most former students of the Polytechnic set up new factories or found jobs in the growing industrial sectors of the region.[25] The possibility of entering entrepreneurial positions was not limited to the sons of businessmen, but was open also to those engineers with managerial skills who were often to be found in the top administrative positions. This is why, after a series of lectures on economics was held by Luigi Luzzatti already in 1866,[26] two important initiatives were taken at the Milan Polytechnic in 1875, both aimed at broadening the preparation of future engineers to the economic field. A series of lectures on Political Economy and Industrial Law were offered that year and two economic courses held by Luigi Cossa, professor of political economy at the university of Pavia, were instituted. A course on political economics and one on industrial economics (one hour per week each) were made compulsory at the third year of the *Scuola di applicazione* for industrial as well as civil engineers. Successively, on a regular basis from 1912, the Milan Polytechnic offered a comprehensive course dealing with law, political and industrial economy in order to broaden the preparation of future engineers.[27]

In England, the engineers became aware of the necessity of a commercial training as the result of the growing pressure of foreign competition that focused attention on cost control and so on 'the economics of engineering'. From the 1870s, various articles in technical reviews (*Engineering, The Engineer*) underlined the importance of the commercial aspects of an engineer's training, and how commercial knowledge was not to be limited to what was commonly known as book-keeping, but should also include a thorough grasp of the principles and practice of prime costing, depreciation, and so on. Recognition was given to the fact that in the great majority of cases the predominant qualification was that of the successful business man, while engineering ability was frequently of a very secondary order and, in some instances, almost entirely supplied by subordinates.

If the first attempts to bridge the gap between the technical and commercial side of the firm, to link the work of engineers with that of accountants, took place from the 1870s in England, many years went by until engineers became regularly instructed in the economic administration of a firm. A first course of lectures was organised by Mather & Platt for members of its staff and given at Manchester in 1917 by Mr. Herbert Casson, the editor of the newly founded *Efficiency Magazine*. The subject of his course was 'the organising side of engineering'.[28] In Liverpool, applied science students were offered facilities to take commercial subjects as an undergraduate study: the fourth year engineering students had to attend six commercial lectures as part of the course.[29]

In 1919 the Institute of Industrial Administration came into being, resulting form the work of an engineer, E.T. Elbourne, who had been in charge of the Ponders End Shell and Gun Factory during the war.[30] While so engaged, he became convinced of the necessity for organising and systematising the administrative duties in such works, and for educating those who had to carry them out. The training of administrators ('those who are responsible for and direct the work of others') was the fundamental object of this Institute.[31] Such training was to be realised in structured courses by correspondence in order to assist intending candidates to obtain the necessary knowledge to sit for examinations. The Institute itself was not responsible for these courses, but gave them its blessing. The examinations in eight groups of subjects were to be held annually.[32] This organisational structure might be included among the causes of its unsuccessful life.

The University of Manchester had made an early start towards a business program when Christie was appointed professor of political economy and commercial science in 1854, with the support of principal Scott who considered the subjects both academically respectable and useful in the area.[33] In 1919 a department of industrial administration was set up at the Manchester College of Technology, while a series of lectures on administration, costing and so on were offered at Bristol University. Before long this was a recognised feature at most of the universities with engineering faculties. King's College School of Engineering at Cambridge adopted a course of lectures in 1929 aimed at awakening the interest of the engineering student to the management problem in industry. After the war, exams on the economics of engineering and engineering management were introduced within the framework of the mechanical and electrical engineers associate membership examinations.[34]

The Higher Schools of Commerce

The Casati Act also established the High Schools of Commerce (later on to evolve into Faculties of Economics).[35] The first *Scuola Superiore di Commercio,* was opened in Venice in 1868, followed by one in Genoa in 1884, one in Bari in 1886 and a private one in Milan in 1902. There were three fields of specialisation: commercial, teaching and consular in preparation for a diplomatic career. Among the promoters of such schools were the major economists of the time: Francesco Ferrara and Luigi Luzzatti in Venice, Gerolamo Boccardo in Genoa, Salvatore Cognetti de Martiis and Maffeo Pantaleoni in Bari.[36]

Italian High Schools of Commerce and British Economics and Commerce Faculties were similar in one respect: in both cases an important milestone in the development of business education was the establishment of accounting courses, which soon spread to the industrial administration field. If the establishment of economics as a major independent university discipline was resisted on various grounds for many years, influenced by businessmen's sceptical attitudes about a discipline developing in a way remote to their comprehension and to their practical needs, accounting soon emerged as an indispensable knowledge for business and industry, requiring specific academic training and thus suitable for elevation to the rank of university subject. From the end of the nineteenth century, many university commerce courses included accounting in their curricula, as it will be shown below.

In 1872, the High School of Commerce in Venice set up the first university chair in accounting (*ragioneria*) and assigned it to Fabio Besta, teacher in the technical institute of Sondrio. Besta believed that the necessary element for the good management of a firm rested upon the importance of efficient economic rules set by the state.[37] Even though industrial administration studies were not advanced at the time, he might well be considered the founder of a new approach to accounting, which was to teach the rules for the good management of enterprises. It was a pupil of Besta, Gino Zappa, who later expanded the subject of accounting to the industrial administration field. As Zappa told the faculty members in 1926

> Accounting is an experimental method with which to investigate the industrial dynamic … There is a strict connection between accounting and industrial administration. Industrial administration is the discipline that investigates how an industry is formed, is bettered and ends, with the aim of improving its management. The study of industrial administration cannot be separated from the study of accounting. The science analysing the life and conditions of an enterprise, the science analysing its industrial administration is thus our science.[38]

Zappa's theory on the evolution of accounting into 'the science of industrial administration' met with severe criticism from his colleagues at the time.[39] This controversy inevitably delayed the progress of management courses inside the High Schools of Commerce. Only in 1934 did *Ca' Foscari* (the High School of Commerce in Venice) began a course of lectures for business managers. The initiative rested upon the Veneto institute for small industry, which financed the project, while *Ca' Foscari* hosted it.[40]

In the *Scuola Superiore di Commercio* in Genoa besides accounting courses (*ragioneria* and *computisteria* which were to be amalgamated in 1905) we find in 1888 a three-year accounting course called *banco modello* having practical purposes, and directed for twenty years (1892–1912) by Lazzaro Ricci. The course focused on mercantile, banking, stock and exchange operations in the first two years, while in the third year students could choose which sector to specialise in. A series of visits to trading and industrial companies was also included. In 1913 the High School of Commerce in Genoa took advantage of the possibility, provided for by a new law on the subject, to set up new *corsi aggregati*. To this end, it introduced a fourth year of study hinged on three fields of specialisation (activated in 1919): industrial economics and administration, customs and transport, and a consular career.[41] In the syllabus for the specialisation in economics and industrial administration we find subjects such as industrial economics and industrial statistics, business administration and accounting for the industrial concerns and technology principles becoming scientific management from 1928. Unfortunately, the specialisation courses did not produce the expected results, registrations fell and the courses were suspended

from 1932. This occurred because: 'the programme of the courses had
become alien to the real problems of the working world, the classes were
held in sporadic ways, and the low standing given to the title by the
industrial-maritime firms ended up with discouraging the students themselves who deserted the fourth year specialisation'.[42]

On the private side, the most important event in management training
was the foundation of the High School of Commerce 'Luigi Bocconi' in
1902, which later evolved into the most famous and prestigious business
school in Italy.[43] It was the intention of its founders, Ferdinando Bocconi (a
businessman) and Leopoldo Sabbatini (secretary of the Chamber of Commerce and entrusted with the task of preparing the syllabus), that the
Bocconi should form a class of people truly learned 'in the economic sciences in order to create the future managers of economic or industrial
enterprises'.[44] Initially, two courses analysing the characteristics of business
administration were offered: political economy principles held by Ulisse
Gobbi of the Milan Polytechnic and general accounting held by Giovanni
Maglione.[45] Yet, the real innovator in the teaching of accounting at the
Bocconi was again Gino Zappa, from the faculty of commerce in Venice. In
1920, an accounting laboratory for technical-commercial research was set
up and entrusted to Zappa. The laboratory was meant to provide solutions
to the problems of costing, accounting, taxable income and balance auditing
of special firms. Zappa also held two courses on accounting and industrial
administration in which he analysed 'the fundamental elements of a firm's
management'.[46] Zappa often referred to real examples in his courses. For
instance through an analysis of some firms' balance sheets, in the conviction
that facts could prove theory and not vice versa.[47]

From a recent study on the sector of activity of Bocconi graduates, it is
apparent that between 1906–39, on average, the great majority were
employed in industrial and business activities (45 per cent), followed by a
high proportion – 28 per cent – in banking, insurance and trading companies.[48] The favourite field of the Bocconi graduate has thus traditionally
been the firm and its administration. In the case of managers coming out
of the Bocconi, it was the school certificate that legitimised their access to
power inside the firm. Once inside a firm, the *Bocconiano* followed a
definite hierarchical path leading to the top administrative positions. In
rare cases, a Bocconi graduate was a 'crown prince'; only 8 per cent were
sons of industrialists.[49] The managment posts most commonly associated
with the *Bocconiano* (general director, managing director, president and
vice-president) were deeply connected with the new structure of joint stock
companies that separated capital from the management of enterprises.
According to the law, it was necessary to possess only a few shares of the
company in order to become managing director, opening the way to the
new figure of manager.

The same development had taken place in Britain from the 1880s, when a general move to limited liability status began, enabling a slow transition from entrepreneurial to managerial capitalism.[50] Yet, at the time, 'the very centre of commerce in the world' was deficient in the means for elevating the character and enlarging the understanding of those engaged in trade and manufacture. At Cambridge, Alfred Marshall was a pioneer in attempting to relate economics to the real world of business and industry: in 1875 he visited the USA and on his return he lectured on American industry and began to write *The Economics of Industry* for the university extension classes. By the 1890s, Marshall had already moved economics much more towards industry and practical affairs. In 'A Plea for the Creation of a Curriculum in Economics', he claimed the need to make economics a separate subject on the grounds that business needed managers specifically trained as such. Marshall obtained the support of business and in June 1903 the honours examinations in economics was instituted and a board of economics and politics was constituted.[51]

The faculty of commerce in Birmingham was the first attempt to provide an education for business management in Great Britain and began thanks to the actions of a single businessman, J. Mason, the largest maker of pen nibs in the world. As one of the founders stated in 1899: 'We desire to systematise and develop the special training which is required by men in business and those who, either as principals or as mangers and foremen, will be called upon to conduct the great industrial undertaking'.[52] This necessity sprang from the consideration that the man of business generally reached the limits of his working life before completing his commercial education. The university would help fill this gap by concentrating the acquisition of such knowledge into a three-year university course. The problem was that of finding a professor to run the commerce courses. W.J. Ashley, teaching at Harvard, seemed to be the solution and was unanimously elected to the post. Ashley had to persuade businessmen, who formed the advisory board, of the value of the course. They were repelled by economics and doubtful of the value of a university course. He emphasised the stimulation that the course would provide and played down the word economics as it caused a 'perceptible chill'. The course, it was stressed, was directed to the training of businessmen not economists.

When the faculty came into being in 1902, business men 'were looking for great things from our Birmingham University. It is of course true that the commercial section cannot turn out business men 'to order'; but by a well-adapted course of training it can bring out latent qualities which otherwise would remain dormant'.[53] Strongly influenced by American attitudes on the relation of higher education and business, Ashley hoped to create 'a university department which might help to produce intelligent and public spirited captains of industry'.[54] He laid considerable stress on foreign languages, commercial law, technique of trade, money, banking and transport, and made accounting part of the course, and the topics covered in his commerce seminar, between 1902 and 1908 ranged widely over industry and commerce. Ashley realised that a means of widening the appeal of the commerce course was his ability to find business openings for the graduates and students who lacked family connections in industry and commerce. To this end, he wrote to local manufacturers and merchants to find positions for particular students: 'I quite expect that before I retire I shall be able to gather round me a room full of managers and managing directors who have been students in the faculty of commerce.'[55] The faculty of commerce at the University of Birmingham was also the first one to provide for a lectureship in accounting.

In London, the evening classes at King's College (where Leone Levi in 1852 began a series of lectures of a practical character on commerce and commercial law),[56] the City of London College and elsewhere, were the only means of practical instruction within reach of the large number of clerks and merchants. The most conspicuous deficiency in London's commercial education was the absence of any provision for higher commercial studies. The parallel at the time was drawn with Paris. Both the *Ecole des Hautes Etudes Commerciales* and the *Ecole Libre des Sciences Politiques* provided a university curriculum as carefully adapted to the needs of the undergraduate who was going to be a leader in business or the official world, as 'the medical faculty does for the undergraduate who is going to be a doctor.'[57] Finally, the need for high commercial and administrative education led to the establishment of the London School of Economics and Political Science in 1895. The aim of the governors was to provide, for the business or official administrator, an education which should be genuinely of university rank, modelled after the Paris example.[58]

The founders of the School contemplated, from the first, the provision of scientific training in the methods of investigation and research, and special courses of study suitable for different groups of businessmen, the civil and municipal services, journalism and public work. The concept of higher commercial education adopted by them was that of a system which should provide a scientific training in the structure and organisation of modern industry and commerce.[59] The School also suggested specific professional curricula for the students who wanted scientific training in accountancy, business and commerce, railway administration, insurance, public and library administration. The school had previously consulted specialists in the various subjects, such as bankers, employers, civil servants, railway administrators and others, in order to throw light on the relation which should have existed between the curriculum offered and the needs of the sector. This collaboration helped the LSE define the training requisite for each specialised field of interest. Therefore, for future railway administrators the teaching of railway economics – held by the School Director W.A.S. Hewins – was an important early element at LSE (together with railway company law, railway statistics and railway law).[60] Also the teaching of accounting and business methods had already started in 1902, the course being held by professor Dicksee.[61] Similar steps were subsequently taken by the universities of Manchester, Liverpool and London.[62] Dicksee's course in accounting was divided into two modules: 'business training from the outset', recommended 'to those who desire to understand how to manage their own affairs, or who look forward to occupying a position of responsibility in any institution or business' and 'business organisation', focusing on the basis of business organisation, the genesis of business enterprise, the elements of finance, business statistics, remuneration of employees, markets, advertising, buying and payments.[63] Besides commerce courses, in both countries it was the subject of accounting that already entailed the provision of proper business knowledge with the aim of preparing future managers.

INITIATIVES FROM THE INDUSTRIAL WORLD

The major driving forces behind the development of business studies, when not the state itself, were often to be found in the business community. In both countries, there are early examples of enlightened entrepreneurs strongly believing that the good running of an enterprise and its industrial competitive efficiency depended upon a full appreciation of the importance of the management function and of the rapid diffusion of management knowledge. Not in a few cases, industrialists' associations and businessmen backed financially the institution of business studies inside the engineering and commerce faculties. After the First World War the impact of scientific management hit both countries to a considerable extent. Not only was a new work organisation introduced inside the firm (time-saving and labour-saving) based on pseudo-scientific taylorist concepts, but management started to be considered as a profession needing specific preparation.

In Italy the industrialists' organisation that stood behind the promotion of management education was the ANFDI (*Associazione Nazionale Fascista Dirigenti Industriali*), an association gathering together the managers of Italian industry. In 1934 the ANFDI signed an agreement with the Milan Polytechnic for an annual contribution of 50,000 *lire* to a post-graduate business course, denominated *Scuola superiore di politica ed organizzazione delle imprese*. ANFDI's commitment was initially set for five years. The aim of the course was to 'improve technical capabilities of managers, and to provide the graduates aspiring to a managing career with appropriate knowledge, enhancing their sense of responsibility to meet the demands of modern industry'.[64] The agreement signed between the Polytechnic and the ANFDI also set the rules for the possible candidates (they had to be professional managers in a firm or graduates in either engineering, chemistry or economics) and established the compulsory subjects. The other subjects to be included in the course, as well as the teaching body, were to be decided by the council of the polytechnic, upon approval by a special joint 'assistance committee' to be set up.

Head of the school was Francesco Mauro, who had introduced the first lectures on scientific management at the Polytechnic in 1928. Source of inspiration for the organisation of the school was the Harvard Graduate School of Business Administration.[65] In order to form the teaching body, Mauro had asked personalities from the intellectual and industrial world to work in his school. A renowned businessman, Alberto Pirelli, was in charge of a course on *teoria della direzione* (theory of management).

At the Turin Polytechnic, it was Fiat's manager Ugo Gobbato who was called upon to hold a four month course on industrial organisation in 1928 (which he held until 1931 when he was sent to work abroad).[66] Gobbato was one of the most interesting examples of an Italian manager with a strong educationalist vocation. When Gobbato was hired at Fiat in 1921, he started his campaign to appropriately educate human resources. In March 1922 Agnelli decided to give credit to Gobbato and set up a school to create the necessary professional capabilities. It turned out to be a very selective three year school for 16–17 years old boys, who would then gain access to technical-administrative tasks, such as store-management and maintenance and repairs jobs.[67] Not surprisingly, when in 1933 Gobbato left Fiat for Alfa Romeo the school closed down. Once in Alfa, Gobbato founded the Alfa school in 1935. The six-month courses aimed at giving university and technical institute graduates a specific knowledge of Alfa's industrial organisation, focusing in particular on the factors of production, technological processes and production costs.[68]

The business-education relationship was more controversial in the case of Britain. Britain's early industrial success had little to do with its educational institutions. As a result, in the nineteenth century British employers demonstrated little interest in formal education, either general or technical, as an asset to young men in business. Learning through practical experience alone was still held to be the best way for young men to learn and prepare themselves for higher posts. If firms resorted to the universities for men, their emphasis was on personality, not formal academic qualifications, in the die-hard conviction that 'managers are born, not made'. But this attitude was no surprise, the parliamentary committee on industry and trade knew perfectly well that businessmen in general did not consider special scholastic training to be useful: 'Such an attitude is not surprising. Many successful business men began business life at an early age and some in a very humble capacity ... [and believe that] to-day, as in the past, competence in business affairs depends very largely upon characteristics of personality'.[69] Even the president of the Association for Education in Industry and Commerce in his 1929 address suggested personality and character as the necessary qualities of the efficient executive: 'Specialised study, and knowledge acquired by experience, may assist in their full development; by themselves they can do but little ... Successful management will always remain the secret of those lucky few who possess the requisite qualities'.[70] This was common thinking among most entrepreneurs. An inquiry conducted by *Business Organisation and Management* in 1926 on how to educate a son for a business career was illuminating. The general advice to entrepreneurs was: 'If your boy is nearly 17, take him away from school at the earliest possible moment. The best years from learning business are those between 17 and 21 ... it is vital that during these years a boy should grasp the sense of "grimness" that belongs to the business world'.[71]

Yet, in Britain, as in Italy, post-graduate business studies were funded by industrialists often under the impulse of an academic personality who had come into contact with the American business education example. One difference that can be highlighted was that whereas in Italy the initiative rested on industrialists associations, in Britain groups of local entrepreneurs often got together in *ad hoc* committees for the financing of a specific initiative. As we have seen, the department of industrial administration at the Manchester College of Technology was started in 1919, after six local companies had been persuaded to fund the initiative. By 1926 the director, J.A. Bowie, had introduced the country's first post-graduate management course.[72] Against the assertion that 'management cannot be taught', Bowie believed that the necessary personal qualities could be developed, refined and canalized by education. Efficiency in industrial management was, therefore, no more a matter of personality than was proficiency in the practice of medicine, law, the church, or teaching. To succeed in industrial life a man needed close familiarity with the technique of management.[73] In 1931, on return from an extensive tour of American business schools, Bowie, as Principal of the School of Economics in Dundee, established a second full-time post-graduate course there in business administration.[74] The other leading department in the subject was opened at the LSE.

As in the case of Manchester, the LSE department of business administration, research and training was established 'at the request and with the support of a number of important business firms' in 1930. The management of the department was in the hands of a joint committee consisting of representatives of the school, of the national institute of industrial psychology, of the Management Research Groups (MRG)[75], and of business firms contributing or subscribing not less than a certain sum to the expenses of the department.[76] Jules Menken, the head of the department, went to Harvard's business school to learn from its experience. The visit was extremely fruitful: the dean of Harvard's business school loaned one of its professors of marketing, and Harvard's volumes of business problems (case studies) were made available.[77] The aim was to develop the study of business administration and the training of men for responsible posts in business. The main teaching work of the department during the experimental period took the form of a one-year course, at postgraduate level. During four years of teaching, nearly seventy-five students took the course, most of them graduates fresh from the universities, the others being non-graduates who possessed some business experience in responsible work. In the teaching work the fullest possible use was made of material drawn from the actual problems and practice of business, the courses being conducted largely in the form of discussion classes, including what was known as the case method. Students visited factories, shops and offices and prepared reports on what they had seen. Discussions, opened by well-known business men, related class work and reading to practical life.

The department also had in operation a scheme for drafting university graduates into business. Firms participating in the scheme selected in any year a man or woman then graduating from a British university and undertook at the time of selection to employ the successful candidate for not less than one year (for a salary of about £200 per annum). Furthermore, a number of well-known men, for the most part representatives of business (Rowntree, Sheldon, Urwick, etc.) assisted the department by participating in a series of informal discussions on various business problems. These discussions took place as rule once a week in the late afternoon and students were expected to attend them as part of their regular work. In 1935, at the end of the five-year experimental period, the governors of the LSE decided to take direct responsibility for the department and to continue and develop it on a more permanent basis as an integral part of the activity of the school, under professor of commerce Arnold Plant.[78] After the war, Plant reopened the post-graduate course with better funding and links, yet it remained a small-scale project. In 1961, not all the twenty-five places were filled and only eight of the students were British. Despite these first efforts to link university work with business demands and form a capable managerial class, the projects often suffered from scarce student participation.

DEBATES IN THE INTER-WAR YEARS

In Italy management issues were debated on the National Board for Scientific Management's (ENIOS) review *L'organizzazione scientifica del lavoro* (OSL). The OSL was the most important vehicle on the Italian scene for the diffusion of the principles of scientific management, their application to single firms, the spreading of the latest news about management techniques, courses on scientific management and national and international gatherings on the issue. Despite the vast popularity enjoyed by the review and its scientific management principles, the turning point in the expansion of the rationalisation drive in Italy was the great depression of 1929. During the early 1930s, rationalisation was condemned for having been one of the causes of the depression.[79] A fiery debate was started in Italy, but the defenders of rationalisation slowly lost ground: ENIOS and the OSL were emptied of all meaning, and management questions lost their grip. Except for a few outstanding exceptions, management training became of only secondary importance. In part the subject did not seem to appeal to businessmen's interest: a typical feature of this inter-war period was the development of technical schools and courses inside the firm to teach technical and managerial tasks to the work-force.[80] Furthermore, the issue was distorted by the fascist philosophy aimed at the creation of a corporate economy led by corporate managers. Francesco Maria Pacces, one of the most active academics in popularising the necessity for management training through a reformed course of university studies, believed that: 'the managing class ... appropriately prepared, would be ready to overcome the difficulties of modern economic life and put the corporative regime of production and distribution into practice'.[81]

During and following the First World War, Britain's approach to scientific management was mediated through the human relations school. The centralising forces in Britain during the war and the management of the war economy had produced contrasting results. Production in state controlled scientifically managed firms started decreasing and a new outlook on the problems of industrial fatigue inaugurated a different approach.[82] Britain's approach to the new American doctrine was thus shaped by its human relations paradigm and by its educational background. British critical attitude was reflected by the fact that scientific management struggled to find enthusiastic emulators among industrialists, eager to incorporate this fundamental feature of American progress into their economic structure.[83] Besides, one of the alleged institutional factors preventing the use of scientific management techniques was 'the scarcity of engineers and their unwillingness to act as advocates of Taylorism'.[84] Yet, it was this somewhat distant and genuine British way to Taylorism that enabled scientific management to not tumble down under the 1929 crisis and enabled management education to remain a greatly debated issue in the inter-war period. The remarkable 1928 Federation of British Industries (FBI) report increasingly recognised the value of industrial administration courses.[85] A revolution was said to have taken place in the conditions of industry and it was plainly evident that the forces affecting industry today are therefore very complex and it may be necessary to scrap old methods of control and management in the same way as it has been necessary to scrap old processes due to the development of scientific discovery. This question of the control and management or administration of industry has gradually evolved as a subject of first importance out of the new conditions of industry.[86]

The 1928 FBI report made clear to possible students (of administration practice) and to educational authorities providing the courses that leadership was a personal factor. If not present, external educational facilities could not provide it. The FBI asserted, however, that modern leadership required knowledge besides personality in the higher ranks of administration.

Another important effort on the part of the business community to foster management training was the attempt made between 1927 and 1930 to set up a British Institute of Management (BIM).[87] In September 1929, Urwick outlined to MRG members the plan for the constitution of a BIM. The draft constitution was subsequently circulated and further considered. The 'Memorandum and constitution for a BIM' focused its attention on the absence in Britain of any co-ordinated national movement for the study and promotion of rationalisation and scientific management. Urwick suggested that the MRG was the most suitable body of organised opinion in the country to initiate such an effort, but the association nearly split under the proposals made. Among MRG members who supported Urwick's idea, it was felt that the better education for management was a pressing need. 'There was a definite need for a body which could effectively interpret industry to education, and which could bring about agreement on the establishment of a set of examinations and degrees, the possession of which would really mean something'.[88] Other MRG members felt that the scheme was premature and were reluctant and sceptical towards the proposal. Mr Tennyson, in pointing out British entrepreneurs' lack of interest in efficiency and better management, accused them of being

inclined to regard the state of British Industry in face of the need for adjusting itself to changed conditions, as somewhat akin to a man standing on the edge of a cold swimming pool, deliberating whether to take a plunge or to wait till he was pushed. The plunge in any case would be precipitate but not premature.[89]

The proposal remained dormant until 1947, when the BIM was finally established.[90]

CONCLUSIONS

Business studies evolved inside higher technical and commercial schools and universities. Italy's relative backwardness in industrial development soon focused public and private attention on the importance of technical education. The well designed Casati law effectively innovated and expanded the provision for technical education. State commitment to higher technical education proved fruitful: enrolments grew and entrepreneurs started looking at industrial engineers and High School of Commerce graduates to fill their managing positions. Normally, both in Italy and Britain students with a degree in engineering often ended up taking care of the administrative side of the firm as well. The Milan Polytechnic was a pioneer in broadening the preparation of its future engineers to 'industrial economics', as the first business courses were called. In commerce faculties, commerce and accounting courses slowly expanded to the industrial administration field, according to the slowly progressing belief that business needed managers specifically trained as such. Technically educated managers with a business specialisation seemed the answer to a firm's needs.

While in Italy state and industry support in the beginning happily combined, assuring a swift development of technical education, in England the country's cultural background was linked to the image of the self-made entrepreneur that had led the industrial revolution and therefore the apprenticeship system was believed to be more important than education in shaping the character of future managers, while technical education was not rated equal with other forms of education which had more social prestige. An arts background was preferred to a technical one for an aspiring manager. Yet, attention to management training was gaining ground in the inter-war period and businessmen's attitudes started to change. Many entrepreneurs recognised that naturally born managers could at least improve their preparation with a specific academic training. Postgraduate courses on management training were set up in various universities and technical colleges with the active support of the entrepreneurial community. The technical college played an important role, since it offered part-time and evening students the opportunity to study management subjects, which soon became very popular. After the Second World War most of the management courses leading to the diploma award of the Urwick scheme were offered in technical colleges.

After the First World War the impact of the American scientific management paradigm hit both countries at the same time and both were influenced by the example set by the American business schools. Most of the personalities involved in the management movement of the two countries had come into contact with American business schools and had been impressed by the progress and the extension of the provision for management education in that country. But it was only after the Second World War that the impact of the American paradigm and the effective impulse given by the National Council on Productivity enhanced the creation of business schools in both countries. As it has been said 'the idea of creating British business schools did not die in these years, largely because of American pressure'.[91] It can in conclusion be stated that the Gerschenkronian 'advantage of backwardness' paradigm springs out very clearly when one compares Britain with Italy: it was the most backward of the two countries that produced a more successful drive towards establishing a formal technical and managerial educational system in support of the more modern sectors of the second industrial revolution.

NOTES

* I would like to thank Terry Gourvish for his support and hospitality at the Business History Unit and Nick Tiratsoo for his precious hints on archive and library material. Finally, I am greatly indebted to Vera Zamagni for her helpful suggestions.

1. See: R.R. Locke, *The End of the Practical Man* (London, 1984); M.B. Rose, 'Beyond Buddenbrooks: the family firm and the management of succession in nineteenth-century Britain' in Browink & M.B. Rose (eds.), *Entrepreneurship, Networks and Modern Business* (Manchester, 1993); M. Sanderson, *The Missing Stratum, Technical School Education in England 1900–1990s* (London, 1994); M.J. Wiener, *English Culture and the Decline of the Industrial Spirit, 1850–1980* (Cambridge, 1981); R. Church, 'The family firm in industrial capitalism: international perspectives on hypotheses and history', *Business History*, Vol. 35 (1993); W.D. Rubinstein, 'Cultural explanations for Britain's economic decline: how true?' in B. Collins & K. Robbins (eds.) *British Culture and Economic Decline* (London, 1990) and J.F. Wilson, *British Business History 1720–1994* (Manchester, 1988), 119.

2. M. Barbagli, *Disoccupazione intellettuale e sistema scolastico in Italia*, (Bologna, 1974).

3. V. Zamagni, *Dalla periferia al centro*, (Bologna, 1991), p. 249.

4. See: G.C. Lacaita, 'L'istruzione tecnica dalla riforma Gentile alle leggi Belluzzo' in Comune di Milano (eds.), *Cultura e società negli anni del fascismo* (Milan, 1987). M. Ostenc, *La scuola italiana durante il fascismo*, (Bari, 1981) pp. 29–30

5. M.J. Bowman and C. Anderson, 'Concerning the Role of Education in Development' in G. Geertz (eds.), *Old Societies and New States* (Glencoe, 1963); L. Sandberg, 'Ignorance, Poverty and Economic Backwardness in Early Stages of European Industrialisation: Variations on Alexander Gerschenkron Grand Theme' *Journal of European Economic History*, Vol. 11 (1982); Locke, *The End of the Practical Man* (London, 1984).

6. The situation facing the newly born Italian government in 1861 was made particularly difficult by the diversity of the educational structures by the

seven different states into which the country had previously been divided and by the deficiencies of some regions' educational provisions. Ten years after unification, there was still extreme disparity in the illiteracy rate between the three regions forming the industrial triangle in Italy (48 per cent) and the South (85 per cent), and a very high national average of 69 per cent; in England those who could neither read nor write only totalled 30 to 33 per cent of the adult population by the middle of the century. See: V. Zamagni, *L'offerta di istruzione in Italia 1861–1987: un fattore guida dello sviluppo economico o un ostacolo?* Università degli Studi di Cassino, Working Paper n. 4 (1993); C.M. Cipolla, *Literacy and Development in the West* (London, 1969), p. 102.

7.   Such professional institutions may be grouped under four different categories covering art, industry, commerce and the education of professional females. See: Zamagni, *L'offerta di istruzione in Italia,* 26. Ministero Agricoltura Industria e Commercio, Ispettorato generale dell'industria e del commercio, 'Notizie sulle condizioni dell'insegnamento industriale e commerciale in Italia ed in alcuni stati esteri' in *Annuario pel 1907* (Rome, 1907).

8.   The Society decided to leave higher technological education to the Polytechnic, concentrating on the provision of technical courses for the working man in order to shape the preparation of juvenile labour according to the demands of industry. After the First World War SIAM opened its first evening technical institute and was able to offer fourteen different courses and schools, some of which were held at weekends, on a number of technical subjects such as mechanics, technical design, mathematics, electricity and weaving. Students attending the different SIAM courses and schools from 1860 to 1945 totalled 141,444. See: C.G. Lacaita, *L'intelligenza produttiva. Imprenditori, tecnici e operai nella Società d'Incoraggiamento d'Arti e mestieri di Milano (1838–1988)* (Milan, 1990), pp. 134, 308–11.

9.   Zamagni, *L'offerta di istruzione in Italia,* 24 ff.

10.   G.W. Roderick and M.D. Stephens, *Scientific and Technical Education in Nineteenth Century England* (Newton Abbott, 1989), pp. 8–9. As Barnes has recently held, in the long run this has meant the triumph of the Oxbridge ideal ('the triumph of tradition') over the civic universities' new model of higher education, which stressed scientific research, practical and professional training. S.V. Barnes, 'Engand's Civic Universities and the Triumph of the Oxbridge Ideal', *History of Education Quarterly,* 36 (Fall 1996), pp. 271–305.

11.   As underlined by Sanderson, the Paris Exhibition contributed to the change in attitude from the antivocational position of British educational institutes to the positive assertion of the rights of the sciences, and even industrial sciences, to be studied in the universities, forging the acceptance of the links binding university and industry. See: Sanderson, *The Universities and British Industry 1850–1970,* pp. 8–14.

12.   The Taunton Report found that 'our industrial classes have not even that basis of sound general education on which alone technical instruction can rest ... our deficiency is not merely a deficiency in technical instruction, but

... in general intelligence, and unless we remedy this want ... our undeniable superiority will not save us from decline'. Public Record Office (PRO), House of Commons (HC) 1871–74 and HC 1882–84; for files relating to the Science and Art Department's grants assigned to the building of new technical institutions see: ED 29 (1860–1904).

13. K. Lysons, *A Passport to Employment. A History of the London Chamber of Commerce and Industry Education Scheme, 1887–1987* (London, 1988), p. 23.

14. On Junior Technical Schools (1913–46) see the files in PRO, ED 98.

15. Sanderson has recently held that this failure to create a stratum of technical education has been a significant element in Britain's relative economic decline since 1900: 'This failure is one of the major defects in English education for it lies at the heart of our neglect in producing the skilled craftsman, artisan and engineer for manufacturing industry'. See: Sanderson, *The Missing Stratum*, p. 1.

16. 'It is to Hogg's patient personal work among working boys that London owes the first model of a Polytechnic Institute'. See: S. Webb, *London Education* (London, 1904), 148–53. See also: Archives of the University of Westminster (AUW), *The Polytechnic of Regent Street, Syllabus and Prospectus 1888–1889*.

17. This remarkable development was rendered possible by the placing on the university level of some of the most qualified polytechnic teachers. Most important of all, duly matriculated students attending their lectures were considered internal students of the university, entitled to proceed, under proper regulations, to the internal degree. Under this constitution more than fifty of the principal teachers of the polytechnics were included in the university, placed on faculties and boards of studies and even elected to the Senate itself. Webb, *London Education*, pp. 168–71.

18. AUW, *The Polytechnic Education Department Prospectuses Session* (hereinafter *Session) 1910–11*.

19. The books for reference were *Shop Management* and *Principles of Scientific Management* by Taylor. In 1925–26 this course changed its name to Economics of Engineering: 'arranged specially to meet the needs of engineers who desire a knowledge of economics as applied to their profession'. AUW, *Session 1925–6*.

20. 'The new science of industrial management is coming to recognise them as that factor in industry which is calling for study and consideration'. See: J. Lee, *Management A Study of Industrial Organisation* (London, 1921), p. 1. This is the first book of a successful series Lee published on the subject.

21. AUW, *Session 1925–26*.

22. AUW, *Session 1930–31*.

23. AUW, *Session 1950–51 Department of Management Studies*.

24. Lacaita, *Istruzione e sviluppo industriale*, p. 125. See also: Guagnini, 'Higher Education and the Engineering Profession in Italy: The Scuole of Milan and Turin, 1859–1914', *Minerva*, 26 (1988), p. 517.

25. On the occasion of the 25th anniversary of the school's foundation, the career patterns that emerge from a survey of the 965 alumni answers shows

clearly that the relative majority of pupils, 210, were engaged in industrial activities; 208 were working as civil engineers; 137 were working in railway societies; 123 in public institutions; sixty-eight in teaching; sixty-seven in provincial technical offices; sixty in private enterprises or public works; thirty-eight ran their own business or a public office; twenty-one were working in insurance companies or rural firms; eighteen were architects and fifteen were in the army. See: C.G. Lacaita, 'La professione degli ingegneri a Milano dalla fine del '700 alla prima guerra mondiale' in A. Martinelli (eds.), *Lavorare a Milano. L'evoluzione delle professioni nel capoluogo lombardo dalla prima metà dell'800 a oggi* (Milan, 1987), 88–9. See also A. Guagnini, 'Academic qualifications and professional functions in the development of the Italian engineering schools, 1859–1914' in R. Fox and A.Guagnini, *Education, technology and industrial performance in Europe, 1850–1939* (Cambridge, 1991), p. 190.

26.   Archivio Politecnico di Milano (APM), file: Luzzatti Luigi, in which there is a letter by Brioschi, dated 6 August 1866, giving notice of the lectures held by Luzzatti on *economia industriale*, which attracted the attention of numerous students.

27.   This course was held by Ulisse Gobbi (rector of the Bocconi University from 1930) until 1934. See: G.B. Stracca, 'La formazione degli ingegneri nel Politecnico di Milano: 1914–63' in E. Decleva, G.B. Stracca and V. Castronovo, *Il Politecnico di Milano nella storia italiana 1914–63* (Bari, 1989), p. 357.

28.   L. Urwick, *The Making of Scientific Management* (London, 1946), pp. 125–6.

29.   Committee on Industry and Trade, *Factors in Industrial and Commercial Efficiency* (London, 1927), pp. 233–6.

30.   In 1919 Elbourne published *The Management Problem* (London, 1919), a record of his war experiences at Ponders End.

31.   'Why was the Institute called the Institute of Industrial Administration and not the Institute of Industrial Management? Elbourne tells me that the matter was carefully considered and the word "administration" chosen because it included not only management but other grades as well', see: R. Sankey, 'IAA *Training for Administration in Industry The Work of the Institute and its Aspirations*', First Presidential Address to the IIA, October 1922 at the LSE, pp. 3–4.

32.   The subjects were: factory planning and plant management; estimating, production methods and rate fixing; production control; employment administration; materials and purchasing; stores and transport management; production statistics and costing. A diploma was granted as a result of examination by the president and the board of management. IIA, *Draft Rules for approval by members at the First Annual General Meeting* (London, 1921), p. 8.

33.   D.R. Jones, *The Origins of Civic Universities* (London, 1988), p. 83.

34.   L. Urwick, *The Making of Scientific Management* (London, 1946), p. 128.

35.   Under fascism, the notorious De Vecchi reform (1934) transformed the High Schools of Commerce in faculties of economics under the supervision of the

Ministry of National Education and local universities, excluding local authorities and chambers of commerce from their administration.

36. Technical school graduates formed the student body of the High Schools of Commerce, whose first problem was the appointment of economics professors. Economics was traditionally taught in the law Faculties and the task of attracting such professors to the new schools was made extremely hard by the disparity in their allowances. While a professor in the Faculty of law earned between 6,000 and 8,000 *lire* in the 1880s–90s, the salary of a High School of Commerce professor ranged between 3,600 and 4,000 *lire*. See: M.M. Augello e M.E.L. Guidi 'I 'Politecnici del commercio' e la formazione della classe dirigente economica nell'Italia post-unitaria' in M.M. Augello, M. Bianchini, G. Gioli, :Roggi, *Le cattedre di economia politica in Italia. La diffusione di una disciplina 'sospetta' 1750–1900* (Milan, 1994).

37. Besta was born in 1845 and from being an elementary school teacher he rose to become teacher in a technical institute and then university professor. Inaugural address by G. Zappa 'Fabio Besta, il Maestro', *Annuario della Regia Scuola in Venezia (ARSV) 1934–35,* pp. 45, 83.

38. Inaugural address by G. Zappa 'Tendenze nuove negli studi di ragioneria' *in Annuario del R. Istituto superiore di scienze economiche e commerciali di Venezia. Anno accademico 1926–26 and 1926–27,* pp. 47–54.

39. De Gobbis and Pacces harshly challenged Zappa on this issue. See: F. De Gobbis 'Tendenze nuove negli studi di ragioneria?' in Regio Istituto Superiore di Scienze Economiche e Commerciali Torino, *Annuario Anno Accademico 1933–34,* 30. F.M. Pacces, *Introduzione agli studi di aziendaria* (Rome, 1935), pp. 80–95.

40. *L'informazione industriale,* 14 April 1935.

41. Massa Piergiovanni, *Dalla Scuola Superiore di Commercio alla Facoltà di Economia* (Genoa, 1992), p. 98–167. Among the teachers in the specialisation course on industrial administration, we find the name of Gino Zappa (1920–21), teaching business administration and accounting.

42. Massa Piergiovanni, *Dalla Scuola Superiore di Commercio,* pp. 171–209.

43. Initially, the new High School of Commerce was to be part of the Milan Polytechnic. In the letter addressed to Colombo and published by *L'industria* on 18 May 1898, Bocconi emphasised the necessity to annex the new school to the Polytechnic 'in order to allow engineering students to attend the classes of the *Istituto Superiore di Commercio* and in the end obtain with the diploma in engineering also the diploma in commerce'. In the end, the 'Luigi Bocconi' was established as an independent private High School of Commerce bearing the name of the son of Ferdinando Bocconi, Luigi, who had perished in the battle of Adua (1896). RITS, *Programma anno 1899–1900,* p. 8.

44. F. Bocconi, 'Per un Istituto Superiore di Commercio in Milano', *Il Sole,* 12 June 1898.

45. Biblioteca Bocconi (B.B.), *Annuario Università commerciale Luigi Bocconi,* issues 1902–14.

46. B.B., *Annuario Bocconi 1922–23,* pp. 44–62

47. In the 1930s management teaching was offered in two courses on *Tecnica*

amministrativa delle imprese industriali and *Scienza dell'economia aziendale*, amalgamated during 1933 into Arnaldo Marcantonio's course on *Tecnica industriale*. B.B., *Annuario Bocconi, 1932–33*.

48. D. Musiedlak, *Université privée et formation de la classe dirigeante: l'example de l'université L. Bocconi de Milan (1902–1925)* (Rome, 1990), own calculations from Table 16, p. 167.

49. Ibid., p. 195

50. As Gourvish has noted, corporate change in Britain before 1914 was more legal and financial than managerial. In fact, the general move to limited liability status did not wholly affect control by founding family groups: in many cases the controlling ordinary share capital was retained by the participating partners and their families. See: T.R. Gourvish, 'British Business and the Transition to a Corporate Economy: Entrepreneurship and Management Structures', *Business History*, 29 (October 1987) p. 24.

51. Sanderson, *The Universities and British Industry*, pp. 198–202.

52. B.M.D. Smith, *Education for Management: its Conception and Implementation in the Faculty of Commerce at Birmingham*, Occasional Paper, Centre for Urban and Regional Studies (London, 1974), pp. 1–10.

53. Ibid., p. 29.

54. A. Ashley, *William James Ashley* (London, 1932), p. 88; and Sanderson, *The Universities and British Industry*, pp. 193–5.

55. Smith, *Education for Management*, pp. 29–31.

56. L. Levi, *Report on Technical, Industrial and Professional Instruction in Italy and other Countries, 1867–1868 to the Right Honourable Lord Robert Montagu, the Vice President of the Committee of Council on Education* (London, 1868), p. 33.

57. London School of Economics and Political Science Library (LSEL), *LSE Calendar for the Session 1909–10*.

58. Webb, *London Education*, pp. 124–5.

59. LSEL, *LSE Calendar for the Session 1903–04*, pp. 19–20; on the history of the LSE see: R. Dahrendorf, *LSE a History of the London School of Economics and Political Science 1895–1995* (Oxford, 1995).

60. LSEL, *LSE Calendar for the Session 1903–04*, pp. 26, 62, 99–100. See also Dahrendorf, *LSE a History of the London School of Economics and Political Science*, p. 21.

61. LSEL, *LSE Calendar 1902–03*. On the subject see also: S. Dev, *Accounting and the LSE Tradition* (London, 1980).

62. S. Nah, *English Accountancy, 1800–1954* (London, 1954), p. 64.

63. The books recommended were Dicksee's *ABC of Bookkeeping* and *Business Organisation*: see the LSE *Calendar for Session 1916–17*, pp. 70–2. Prof. LR Dicksee published 27 books on accounting problems (between 1892 and 1932). His *Office Organisation and Management* introduced his students to a new conception of clerical methods and equipment. His *Business and Organisation*, first published in 1910, was a book considerably in advance of the general practice of the time.

64. APM, Corso Mauro, Convenzione con il R. Istituto Superiore di Ingegneria (Politecnico di Milano), 20 April 1934.

65. F. Mauro, *Gli Stati Uniti d'America visti da un ingegnere* (Milan, 1945).

66. On Gobbato see: Archivio Storico Fiat (ASF), File Ugo Gobbato.

67. ASF, Giuseppe Berta, *La scuola allievi Fiat*, p. 9–23.

68. Centro di documentazione storica Alfa Romeo (CSDAR or Alfa Romeo Archive), Direzione generale 9 maggio 1941 'Funzionamento della Scuola Interna "Alfa"'.

69. Committee on Industry and Trade, *Factors in Industrial and Commercial Efficiency*, p. 220–1.

70. The Association for Education in Industry and Commerce, *Eleventh Annual Conference*, London July 1929, AEIC Birmingham. Presidential Address by Sir M.J. Bonn 'Towards Education at the Top', 9–13.

71. 'How shall I Educate My Son for a Business Career? An Enquirer Obtains the Opinions of Several Business Men', *Business Administration and Management*, 13 (March 1926), p. 306.

72. C. Wilson, *The Manchester Experiment: a History of Manchester Business School, 1965–1990* (London, 1992), pp. 2–3.

73. J.A. Bowie, *Education for Business Management* (Oxford, 1930), p. 45.

74. 'No one can visit these large American schools of business without feeling some misgivings on the industrial future of any country which lacks them'. J.A. Bowie, *American Schools of Business* (London, 1932), p. 10. See also: J.A. Bowie, 'American Developments in Education for Industrial Management' in E.T. Elbourne (eds.), *Fundamentals of Industrial Administration. An Introduction to Management* (London, 1947). L. Urwick, *The Golden Book of Management, A Historical Record of the Life and Work of Seventy Pioneers*, (London, 1956).

75. The main idea underlying the formation of these Groups in 1926 was organised cooperation between a number of businesses in the solution of their common problems of management and of administration. The object of a Group was to assist specialists to keep in closer touch with their subjects by mutual help. See, Management Research Groups, *What they are and how they work*, Williams & Norgate Ltd, Covent Garden, No.1, July 1927. Hon. Secretary L.Urwick, pp. 4–5.

76. LSEL, *LSE Calendar Session 1930–31*, p. 387.

77. S. Keeble, *The Ability to Manage. A Study of British Management, 1890–1990* (Manchester, 1992), p. 116.

78. LSEL, *LSE Calendar Session 1935–36*, pp. 261–9.

79. See the article on *OSL* March 1931 on the 'limits of rationalisation', where it was held that in the case of an overpopulated country, characterised by low salaries, rationalisation was an economic nonsense. See also the reply by G.Ottone 'Considerazioni a proposito dei limiti della razionalizzazione' *OSL*, 6 (June 1931) p. 256.

80. Archivio Generale Confindustria, Fondo Istruzione Professionale.

81. F.M. Pacces, 'Per un'università degli studi economici', *Civiltà Fascista*, 12 (1933) pp. 1069–70. In 1929 Pacces also planned the constitution of 'The Italian management institute', which remained on the paper until the postwar period.

82. The management strategies of Quaker entrepreneurs such as Rowntree, Owen

and Cadbury, pioneers in the human relations approach, had displayed a British lack of confidence in how the American systems treated labour already before the war. Quaker entrepreneurs had always taken a leading role in demanding that employers acknowledge and tolerate their social obligations. Administration in Quaker factories had always attempted to follow the ethical precept of the kindly spirit. Rowntree's writings were centred on the social obligations of industry to labour: 'We owe it to the workers that the material conditions under which they work shall be satisfactory.' At the close of the First World War, many British employers were beginning to recommend many of the same methods, recognising them to be technically, as well as morally, valuable. See: B.S. Rowntree, 'Social obligations of industry to labour', *Industrial Administration. A Series of Lectures* (Manchester, 1920), p. 10; L.Urwick, 'The development of scientific management in Great Britain', *British Management Review*, 3 (October – December 1938) p. 43.

83. On the issue see: F. Fauri, 'Istruzione e governo dell'impresa', Bologna, 1998.

84. M.F. Guillén, *Models of Management. Work, Authority, and Organization in a Comparative Perspective* (Chicago, 1994), 213 ff.

85. Modern Record Centre Warwick (MRC), MSS 200 /F/3/T2/2/2 FBI Minutes of the second meeting of the London education sub-committee of the FBI July 1928.

86. MRC, MSS 200 /F/3/T2/2/2 FBI 'Education in relation to industrial administration'. Report of 1928.

87. Barnes, *Managerial Catalyst: the Story of London Business School 1964 to 1989* (London, 1989), 14–15.

88. LSE Archive (LSEA), MRG BOX 106, Mr Renold intervention in MRG No.1 'British Management Institute Appeal 1930'.

89. Ibid., Mr Tennyson intervention.

90. After the war the BIM met with diffidence, if not open hostility: 'The Government's announcement that it was to form the BIM met with a great deal of enthusiasm in some management movement circles ... others felt that if the State was involved private enterprise would be inevitably threatened. In this situation, organisations such as the Industrial Management Research Association (IMRA previously Management Research Groups) began lobbying to minimise the BIM's status and impact.' See: N. Tiratsoo, 'Standard Motors 1945–55 and the Post-war Malaise of British Management' in Y. Cassis, F. Crouzet, T. Gourvish, *Management and Business in Britain and France. The Age of the Corporate Economy* (Oxford, 1995), p. 106.

91. N. Tiratsoo, 'Management education in post-war Britain' in V. Zamagni, L. Engwall, *Management Education in an Historical Perspective* (Manchester, 1998).

Conflicting Logics in the Formation of the French Pharmaceutical Industry 1803–1959

Michèle Ruffat

Institut d'Histoire du Temps Présent, Centre National de la Recherche Scientifique, Paris

INTRODUCTION

The development of the pharmaceutical industry in France bore for a century and a half the strong imprint of the rigid regulatory framework set up under the Empire. The Napoleonic regime encouraged science and, with the so-called 'Germinal law'[1] of 1803, sought to raise the level of training of pharmacists and to combat obscurantist therapeutic practices. The granting of a monopoly, in exchange for the setting up of a genuine profession to be practised only by those whose skills were sanctioned by a diploma, cleaned up the trade in medicines. However, it was a measure conceived only to regulate the exercise of a craft-based activity, and as such it had adverse effects on later developments: by prohibiting 'secret' remedies, which had given free reign to charlatanism, it also barred the road to innovation. Only drugs registered in the Codex, which were sanctioned by custom and experience, were legal. Pharmacists had sole responsibility for the manufacture of drugs in their dispensaries, thus excluding associations with third parties and the introduction of outside capital.

The Germinal law therefore regulated the profession as it stood at the beginning of the nineteenth century. It froze its operations within rules that were suitable to traditional practice, but which were to shackle the development of the French pharmaceutical industry for almost a century and a half. Until the passing of the 1941 law which established an official visa for pharmaceutical products and granted them minimal protection from counterfeiting, and the 1959 law on special pharmaceutical patents, pharmaceutical innovation was supposed to fall into the public domain as soon as it occurred. This static regulatory context had a long-term impact on the strategies and structures of French pharmaceutical firms, until those changes in the legislative framework enabled them to adapt to the exponential growth in health spending in post-war France.[2]

THE LEGISLATIVE FRAMEWORK

The establishment of a monopoly of the manufacture and sale of medicines in 1803 at last met the demands of a profession which had had great
difficulty in establishing its autonomy from doctors, who had long dis-
pensed their own recommended remedies, the clergy, and raw materials
stockists, whether herbalists, grocers or ironmongers, not to mention ped-
dlers and tinkers of every sort. The law sought to remedy the chronic ills
associated with the practice of an art which was mocked by Molière in his
play *Le Malade Imaginaire* and was much discredited under the Ancien
Régime. The abuses that arose from the uncontrolled sale of medicinal or
supposedly medicinal products, the multiplication of dangerous substances
due to advances in chemistry and the necessity, in public health terms, to
restrict administration to optimum doses, had finally made the case for the
pharmacist monopoly.

The Germinal law, inspired above all by the fight against the charlatanism
and greed that had characterised the trade in medicines under the Ancien
Régime, sought to clarify the situation and protect the population by
restricting the manufacture and sale of drugs to the pharmacist profession.
In return for this monopoly, the law required competence: a diploma was
needed in order to practise as a pharmacist. As a consequence, the professional had to be the absolute master of his dispensary, for which he was
solely and totally responsible: hence the prohibition of any partnership
between qualified and unqualified people in the running of a dispensary. It
was a wise measure at the time, but its effect was to institutionalise a non-
industrial mode of operation. When the law was passed, it ruled that the
pharmacist, who exercised his art by making all the products he sold, had
the essential task of preparing raw materials of plant or mineral origin,
whose therapeutic activity was recognised and listed in the Codex and
whose formula was prescribed by the doctor. The law conceived this
activity as essentially static, and made no provision for change in its
principle or in its methods. It prohibited as 'secret remedies', and hence a
priori suspect, all medicines not listed in the Codex, i.e. all those whose
formula was not known, listed and approved by the medical authorities,
habit and experience. Inscription in the Codex was a way of insuring that
effective preparations would not be restricted to the rich and powerful, or
be lost with the inventor, and that medicine, a shared resource of humanity, could not be monopolised for one person's profit.

The Germinal law thus ratified the state of the profession as it stood at the
time. It made no distinction between the production and sale of medicines,
since these functions were not differentiated in the traditional dispensary.
However, a specialisation of the two activities became inevitable with the
onset of industrialisation. The share of magistral preparations inexorably

fell during the nineteenth century with the growth of 'brand medicines', due to both technical and commercial factors. 'The preparation or refinement of recent remedies', reported the trade press in 1910, 'requires a set of operations and devices that can only exist in industry'.[3] Pharmacy was entering a new era, where the progress of chemistry and medicine would combine to rationalise traditional practices and explore new avenues.

The law had long-lasting consequences. In France, the dispensary and the pharmaceutical firms would remain linked, by contrast with other countries where the latter emerged from the chemical industry. By theoretically banning pharmacists and non-pharmacists running a dispensary as a partnership, it imposed the rule of self-financing and closed the profession to outside investors. As a result, every pharmaceutical firm was subject to the same legal rules as the dispensary.

The need to find start-up funds was nothing new for pharmacists. Expedients were found in the 19th century. To attain the paradise of the dispensary, joked a contemporary humourist, it was often necessary to pass through the purgatory of marriage. 'Find me a wife', begs an impecunious pharmacist of the boss he aspires to succeed ... 'The latter gets to work, negotiates with a bourgeois family from a neighbouring town, stipulates the terms of the contract, and two months later his pupil accompanies to the town hall a young person he has met twice before, and who arrives by stagecoach to promise him eternal fidelity. The dowry had paid for the pharmacy'.[4]

But the needs of the industry were on a different scale. Beyond the initial start-up period when pharmaceutical firms were former dispensaries that had prospered through the launch of pioneering products, the industrial scale manufacture of medicines necessitated investment. Where would capital come from? And how could innovation develop in a legal context that offered no protection for it, since inscription in the Codex, the necessary step for marketing pharmaceutical products, implied the immediate transfer of their formulae to the public domain?

IMPLEMENTATION OF THE GERMINAL LAW

Confronted with the necessity of adapting to that legal framework, which was hampering their development, pharmaceutical firms commonly took one of the three following positions: compliance, alliance or avoidance, with various degrees of success and long-range consequences for the strategy and structure of the French pharmaceutical industry.

Compliance

Strict compliance proved difficult. Of course, self-support was the rule for small business at the time, but family resources or profits from the activity of a traditional dispensary, however successful, were hardly sufficient to finance the setting up of manufacturing facilities. In the nineteenth century, colleagues were no more inclined than other French savers to invest in industry, even their own. 'It is suggested that pharmacists might play a more active part in the industrial and commercial firms in their sector', stated the trade press at the beginning of the century ... 'Unfortunately, the industry requires significant funds, and pharmacists prefer to buy their annuity through the state, gold mines or prize bonds'.[5] Besides, dispensary pharmacists saw no reason to invest in an activity that they felt was in competition with their own. France was a nation of thrifty savers, and borrowing was not among the mores of the time, while the banks were not keen to take risks by lending to firms of modest size.

However, for Amans Dausse,[6] a manufacturer of plant extracts to be used by pharmacists to make magistral preparations and a pharmacist himself, the pharmaceutical monopoly was an article of faith. Family management by pharmacists was the rule, and the founder's daughter, granddaughter and great-granddaughter obliged by marrying pharmacists. Five generations followed each other at the helm. When Laboratoires Dausse later chose to admit pharmacist shareholders to the capital inherited by the two brothers Émile and Édouard Boulanger-Dausse through an opening of capital, it was as much a marketing operation as a financial one. A joint stock company was founded in 1930, but the brothers continued to hold a large majority (71 per cent) of the shares, essentially corresponding to their contribution of trademarks with an estimated value of 7.8 million French Francs out of a total corporate value of eleven million French Francs. Thus Dausse opened the capital to some 600 pharmacists.

This new shareholding structure showed a willingness to open up to a significant, but restricted, number of colleagues, each investing amounts that were modest, even nominal, yet which would create special links with a company whose products they knew well and would promote. The pattern proved very stable. Eight years later, in 1938, the company still had about the same number of shareholders. It had bet on the trust of the 'great pharmaceutical family', but remained under the control of the heirs. Dausse maintained, come hell or high water, its attachment to the traditional 'pharmaceutical only' shareholding, even after the passing of the 1941 law that made partnerships between pharmacists and non-pharmacists acceptable under certain conditions.

In the wake of that operation, Laboratoires Dausse launched a promotional campaign in the 1930s aimed at pharmacists alone. In fact, it introduced a new method of commercialization, whereby pharmacists already selling the firm's products were to promote them to other dispensaries within their radius of operations. A 1933 circular reads:

For 25 years, the house of Dausse has worked to perfect a large number of galenic products, without losing sight of its goal, which is the scientific study of the Extract, for its application to therapy … We did not seek to make brand medicines, but all our trademark products were delivered, in bulk, to drug manufacturers wishing to profit from our discoveries and from the care that goes into our products … We have produced a large number of galenicals and many of them are still in stock … It would be a complete impossibility to make all of them known to the medical profession … that is why we are addressing ourselves to our many pharmacist friends so that they can profit from this unproductive stock. We are offering you a programme which will make it possible to eliminate some medical publicity and replace it with your personal propaganda amongst your medical entourage.[7]

A 'special stockist-seller' licence was proposed, based on the following argument:

What is the most important factor in the cost of a brand medicine? … It is medical publicity, which is becoming increasingly costly and increasingly ineffective as the numbers of brand medicines increase. Can part of this advertising be economised? … Yes, if the person who supplies the medicine agrees to promote it effectively to doctors, whom he sees frequently, and to provide them with literature and samples … We believe that the savings achieved by this form of promotion represent some 20 per cent of the price of the product sold to the pharmacist, who will thus profit from the savings.

It was emphasised that any public advertising in the daily papers or on posters was forbidden and that advertisements in the medical press were to be submitted to Laboratoires Dausse for approval.

This proposal is indicative of the quality of the links between Dausse and dispensary pharmacists, who received preferential treatment when they were shareholders, debenture loan subscribers or concessionaires. It also highlights the problems caused by the multiplication of brand medicines and presentations, and the impossibility of keeping track with equivalent levels of product advertising. It was also a response to the years of economic crisis, which led to an 18 per cent drop in turnover between 1930 and 1933 and staff reductions for Dausse of 30 per cent in Paris (from 194 to 138 head office personnel) and eleven per cent (from 220 to 196) at their plant in Ivry in the outskirts of Paris. In the 1950s, as the number of stockholders started to fall, Laboratoires Dausse modified the rigid provisions which restricted stockholding to pharmacists alone. At the annual shareholders' meeting of 28 November 1957, 16 years after it became possible, it was decided that share ownership would no longer be restricted to qualified pharmacists.

So Dausse did manage to grow for more than a century within the strict limitations of the law. But it was a manufacturer who had to maintain its image as a pharmacist for its clients and thrived on it. The processes it had developed guaranteed the quality of the products it made and could be protected by patents.

Alliance

Other entrepreneurs in the field explored the possibilities that alliances with related businesses, which were not constricted by the same rules, could offer.

Robert & Carrière's business was focused from the start on the exploitation of a sterilisation process, which was made possible by an initial partnership between the pharmacist Joseph Robert and an industrialist, Paul Carrière, a wax and candle maker, for the creation of the 'Laboratoire de stérilisation par les procédés Robert & Carrière'.[8] Paul Carrière made available to Joseph Robert his Bourg-la-Reine factories, which were only relinquished in the late 1950s. As for the 'société anonyme des Laboratoires Robert & Carrière', the new legal structure adopted in 1921, its registered function was 'the sale of all products relating to hygiene, chemistry, etc.'.[9] It could not at the time include the manufacture of pharmaceutical products, which remained theoretically – although case law was showing itself increasingly tolerant – the prerogative of pharmacists alone. However, when Mr. Carrière left the board of directors in 1922, he was replaced by a pharmacist, which showed the growing importance of brand medicines in the firm's output in relation to medical and surgical equipment. The company was weary of raising new capital in the stock market. In 1930, the board of directors laid down the principle that 'the company must be able to live by its own means without ever having recourse to outside money'.[10] It was not until 1945, shortly after the 1941 law permitted association with non-pharmaceutical capital, that the first capital increase took place.

Avoidance

During the 19th century, as the rationalisation of manufacturing processes, which incorporated recent advances in chemistry and physics and moved the profession towards full-scale industrialisation, led to an inexorable reduction in the role of magistral preparations in favour of ready-to-use 'specialities', the industry found itself obliged to seek its right to legal existence outside the rules specific to the profession.

While the 1844 law on patents declared pharmaceutical compositions non-patentable, the industry found its charter and its manoeuvring space in the 1857 law on trademarks. According to it, the brand or trademark was lawful and consequently had a right to the protection of the law against counterfeiting. Pharmaceutical products were not excluded, as long as the brand name was not the same as the name of the product itself, which would have been equivalent to granting an individual the privilege of sole rights to and profit from the remedy, as ownership of the brand would tend to confer a monopoly over the product.[11]

Thus the 1857 law laid down in principle the independence of the trademark and the product. It followed that while the manufacturer or the seller of brand medicines was always obliged to be a qualified pharmacist, the owner of the brand did not need to be. This meant that the owner could be a legal entity, for example a company, which would be free to attract the capital required for the expansion of the business.[12] The industrialisation of drug production would often employ this particular legal arrangement between two firms, whereby one would own the brands, and the other, necessarily headed by a qualified pharmacist, would be fully responsible for manufacturing the products under a licence granted by the first in return for royalties.

Thus, the pharmaceutical industry was able to grow through a combination of the provisions of the Germinal law and those of the trademark law. 'Had the 1857 law not been interpreted in this way', notes François Prevet, a lawyer and pharmacist, 'there would have been no French pharmaceutical industry'.[13]

The consequence was the superabundant and somewhat disordered proliferation of maker's brand pharmaceutical specialities which arose out of the legal vacuum left by the growing obsolescence of the Germinal law. Trademarks were a very valuable asset. When Robert & Carrière was incorporated in 1921, the capital of 3.5 million francs was divided into 7,000 shares of 500 francs each, and the founders received 4,000 shares in remuneration of the trademarks registered by the firm in its first quarter century of existence.

In fact, this generalisation of the trademark was not specific to pharmacy. As a means of recognising and identifying products, and particularly their quality, they were coming out of every industry and invading every trade, from engineering and food to general stores. That is why the pharmaceutical firms gave their products names that recalled the company name itself. Hence the systematic use of the suffix *dausse* for products of the Laboratoires Dausse (*camphodausse*, *prostatidausse*, *sérodausse*) and the registration of the Ercé brand (the phonetic transcription in French of Robert & Carrière's initials RC, used since the beginning of the century and still to this day, from Ercé grey oil, the antisyphilitic launched in 1905, to the Ercéfuryl sold today).

The pharmaceutical product fitted the trademark mould all the more easily in that the trend at the time was towards the mass market, sustained by advertising, rather than the so-called 'ethical' market, dependent on medical prescription alone. The yoke imposed on the profession by the Germinal law led paradoxically to the unlimited freedom of the pharmaceutical firms through trademark companies. The consequence, according to the Robert & Carrière board in 1934, was 'the plethora of new brand medicines' which made it necessary to 'multiply propaganda efforts'.[14] In all, the number of products for sale was around 20,000, i.e., five times more than today.

Advertising certainly played a very important role in the marketing process. Robert & Carrière's advertising budget, modest in the 1920s, shot up in the following decade both in France and abroad to reach 15 to 25 per cent of turnover. A prestige brochure, *Les Deux Ciels*, 'much appreciated by the elite to whom it was addressed', which placed the firm under the double aegis of Pascal and Pasteur, was printed in 15,000 copies in 1931. It was distributed to doctors, to whom information on the drugs was exclusively addressed.

Other changes in business law eased the way for pharmaceutical firms. The use of the *société anonyme* [limited liability company], which was permitted without authorisation from 1867, proved a preferable way of obtaining fresh money. Here, the associates were a party to the venture at their own risk, and could not insist on repayment of their funds. Although the Germinal law laid down the principle of the pharmacist's full and exclusive responsibility, the courts, when confronted with the actual practice of establishing links with other more or less related activities, were increasingly careful not to take a position on the heart of the matter.[15] In the 1930s and 1940s, many firms adopted the legal status of a SARL [private limited liability company], which had been instituted in 1925 and was ideally suited to offer a flexible framework for family firms with a small number of shareholders possessing complementary skills who knew each other well.

The Germinal law was bypassed in other ways. In theory, the prohibition on 'secret remedies' stayed in force and all innovation was supposed to go straight into the public domain. However, the State implicitly recognised infringements of this principle by introducing a tax on products sold without their composition being shown. In 1916, an initial tax of 6 per cent was applied to brand medicines whose formula did not feature on the packaging. A further law of 1926 taxed products advertised to the public and exempted those limited to technical, medical or pharmaceutical advertising. Finally, in 1935, all pharmaceutical specialities were subjected to a single tax. This was how in various ways, 'to protect public health, the Germinal law instituted an apparent privilege for the pharmacist (the monopoly) but under conditions that placed him outside the common law'.[16] Increasingly, in the inter-war period, 'lawyers had to work hard indeed not to dig too deep a ditch between fact and law'[17] as pharmaceutical laboratories multiplied in a legal framework that addressed problems of the past.

CONSEQUENCES FOR THE STRATEGY AND STRUCTURE OF THE
PHARMACEUTICAL INDUSTRY

Those roundabout methods of survival stamped the industry with characteristics that were to mark its development for a long time to come.

Concentration on processes rather than products

Some firms chose to make their best innovative efforts on processes, which
were patentable. Robert & Carrière and Dausse, for example, had in
common that their businesses were founded on the exploitation of processes rather than products, the first for the sterilisation of surgical equipment, the second for the manufacture of plant extracts for the preparation
of medicines in the dispensary. The law thus allowed them to register their
processes and thus protect their know-how. When their financial viability
and their social purpose were secured on those bases, they could start the
production of pharmaceutical specialities with all due caution.

Orientation of innovation toward improvement in galenical forms

In the inter-war period, therapy lived very much by its own momentum.
The family doctor of the 1920s and 1930s had at his disposal no more
than half a dozen medicines aimed at specific diseases.[18] Of these, quinine
for malaria and 'fevers' and ipecacuanha for dysentery were drugs as old
as time, the first brought back from Peru in the 17th century by the Jesuits,
who got it from the Indians, the second from Brazil in the 16th century.
The third – digitalis or foxglove – was a remedy in use since the 18th
century for certain cardiac conditions, and the fourth, mercury, used for
the treatment of syphilis, was an ancient remedy from Hindu medicine,
rediscovered in the Middle Ages by an astrologist versed in the occult
sciences.

Most drugs, at that time, were applied to a wide variety of disorders.
Quinine was prescribed in turn for infectious illnesses, colds, skin diseases,
anaemia and neuralgia. Potassium iodide was used as a universal remedy
for age related disorders like high blood pressure, heart conditions, obesity
and digestive problems. Iron was prescribed for anaemia, the illness of the
times, but also for tuberculosis, kidney troubles and arthritis, and bicarbo-
nate of soda for all digestive conditions, including those caused by infec-
tion, while belladonna was given equally for the eyesight and for
constipation.

The only really 'modern' drugs, i.e., drugs acting as 'magic bullets'
aimed at the causes of specific conditions, were the arsenobenzenes, which
destroyed the syphilis bacterium. These were discovered by Paul Ehrlich at
the end of the nineteenth century, and earned him the Nobel Prize for
medicine in 1908. In addition, a few vitamins were beginning to be prescribed as a remedy for specific deficiencies. Most of the known drugs,

though not necessarily ineffective, had emerged out of an accumulation of empirical observations, in other words from 'the art of healing without knowing exactly what, or exactly why'.[19]

In that context, real innovations were few and far between, nor were they encouraged by the legislative framework, which was traditionally more preoccupied with keeping fraudulent drugs out of the market than by promoting research of new drugs. So many French drugmakers resorted to improvements in the presentation of existing products, to make them more convenient to use. When in 1945 Paul Métadier looked back over his half-century of involvement in the pharmaceutical industry, he observed that although 'the whole of France gained from the excellent reputation of our pharmaceutical specialities, so ingeniously presented, assuredly not all of them represented sensational innovations'.[20] It is true that in that period, the creativeness of French pharmacy showed itself more through the quality and diversity of presentation of its drugs and their export success than through fundamental discoveries. This period of relative latency in creativity led French pharmaceutical firms between the wars to specialise on the search for ever more refined and subtle forms of presentation, which were the source of their strength and their reputation outside France and ensured their penetration into foreign markets.

Externalisation of innovation on pharmaceutical products

An instigator of the future reforms wrote in 1937:

> Let us suppose, that a doctor, for example – it is a common case –, discovers a new product which represents a major therapeutic advance. He can neither patent his discovery[21] nor protect it with a trademark, for a pharmaceutical trademark is null if it applies to a new product[22] ... the pharmaceutical product never becomes the property of its inventor, even if he has spent his whole life researching it ... as soon as it takes form, as soon as its existence has been disclosed even if it has not left the laboratory or been given a name, it escapes from its creator who will never be able to claim the exclusive right to make it.[23]

This meant that the inventor's natural partner was the pharmaceutical firm. In each number of the review *L'Asepsie*, which Robert & Carrière published in the 1920s, there is an insert in bold characters entitled 'Important Notice', which reminds its physician readers that 'our laboratories and workshops are always entirely at their disposal for the study and manufacture of all new products or devices'. The pharmaceutical firm acted as a pole of attraction where potential products were sorted, developed and tested. Doctors formed from their practice ideas for improvements to products and processes which could only be translated into reality through testing and production by suitably equipped pharmaceutical firms.

The quantity and quality of the proposals that came into pharmaceutical firms depended on their reputation and the distribution of their products. The only way an inventor had a chance of seeing his product on the market was by an agreement with one of them. In 1927, of the 33 new products – mostly surgical instruments or devices for patient examination – announced to Robert & Carrière shareholders, a good half were named for the physician who invented them.[24] 'Most of these novelties', it was specified, 'were made entirely in our workshops. Others were brought to us spontaneously because of our firm's great reputation: among these, we would mention the Weil and Dufourt vaccine which, in a few months, has taken a significant place in our business'.[25]

Those arrangements were frequent causes of severe conflicts. When Professor Félix Hubert d'Hérelle, a Canadian doctor and microbiologist, entrusted the manufacture of bacteriophages[26] to Robert & Carrière, following his 1917 discovery with E. Vollman of the phenomenon of microbial lysis, Professor d'Hérelle granted an exclusive contract for France to Robert & Carrière, which launched the Laboratoire du bactériophage and shared the profits with the inventor. In the 1930s, it was one of the firm's top half-dozen products. On the heels of this success, Professor d'Hérelle sought to go back on the contract in order to obtain better terms. The outcome eventually went the company's way. But the battle demonstrated the significant shortcomings of industrial property law in that field.

Further collaborative links were created between laboratories and the hospital sector, since clinicians held the keys to experimentation on new products. Indeed, the foundations of the mutual trust were laid during student days, for – a positive consequence of the Germinal and the 1941 law – the quality of pharmacy studies rose steadily to the same level as medical training, with treatment naturally seen as the field of the pharmacist. The hospital internship was often the place where professionals from complementary disciplines met and established links and shared working habits that would bear fruit in the future. By these means, each pharmaceutical firm created a network of practitioners who offered collaboration before and after the launch of new products.

'A large number of inventors', stated a 1926 Robert & Carrière report to shareholders, 'have entrusted their devices to us for development and often improvement in our workshops, or have simply brought us designs that we have produced and perfected in our laboratories'.[27] What was brought to the company was often an idea for a product, or an observation that might lead to a medicine. These contributors were to receive 'author's royalties' and were paid a percentage of sales, of the order of 10 per cent, which bound them to the manufacturers by giving them an interest in the commercial success or failure of the product. These arrangements were often informal and precarious, and this, in the legal vacuum where innovation took place, gave rise to conflicts which could affect the smooth progress of affairs.

In that respect, Robert & Carrière did not escape the consequences of gaps in the law as regards industrial property. It was to experience a serious crisis in its early years as a result of the absence of regulation in this area. The idea of Stannoxyl, a tin based product used to treat furonculosis, was brought to the company by a chemist who had observed that workers in the tin trade seemed to be exempt from the disease. Robert & Carrière had registered the trademark for this product, which was a success and played a role in the setting up of the company in 1921.

Hardly was the company set up than the chemist claimed full ownership of the trademarks and, on the basis of post-war inflation, demanded the doubling of the royalties he had agreed to receive under the terms of the 'obscure and constantly modified' contract signed in 1917. There followed an expedition to the plant in Bourg-la-Reine where he 'arrived one morning by car and carried off products being processed for the preparation of rare-earth salts with the purpose of hindering our production'.[28] The resulting lawsuit was won, as it happens, by the company, but it illustrated the perils of the only recourse possible 'to known customs generally applied in similar circumstances', in the absence of legislation establishing the respective rights of the parties.

Another bone of contention was the recourse to the 'secret patent' filed in a company's name. This was a 'sealed registration' system which made it possible to set a date for the invention of a product, which could be used against later claims. But in-house research was not a core activity anyway. The essential tasks, in most pharmaceutical firms of the time, remained the monitoring of raw materials, the control and improvement of manufacturing processes, testing and development of potential new products proposed to them, and quality control.

Conflict of interest between traditional pharmacists and pharmaceutical firms.

The 'brand medicines quarrel', which in the nineteenth century was the source of a harsh struggle between proponents of magistral preparations and partisans of industrial drug production, was still raging in the inter-war period. It took the form of conflicts on prices, which would culminate in cut-throat competition and spendings on publicity that made pharmacy the number one contributor to the finances of the press.

The intense domestic competition on prices created an impetus towards the conquest of external markets. In the inter-war period, pharmacists were free to set their prices to the public. New products, launched to much publicity, were thus a way of distancing oneself from similar products and of restoring profit margins eroded by competition. The fall in prices was also the consequence of fratricidal competition between dispensaries and pharmaceutical firms in a fast changing profession.

> Initially, brand medicines were rare and magistral preparations were the rule. The prices of brand medicines were therefore reduced to attract prescriptions. When the profit on these drugs fell to near zero, and sometimes even below zero, the necessity for regulation was admitted. Subsequently, when brand medicines became as common as the magistral preparation was rare, the prices of the latter fell to attract potential buyers of brand medicines into dispensaries.[29]

This downward spiral created a constant incentive to launch new 'specialities' that would pay their way on profitable external markets.

THE REFORM OF THE LAW

By the end of the 1930s, the profession was in crisis: 'In 1938', wrote Paul Métadier, a tenor of the profession,[30] 'the severe crisis that had long been raging accentuated the contradiction between the Germinal law and reality 135 years later. There was confusion and disorder in every aspect of our business ... Our discipline had lost its legal and professional foundations'.[31] The gap between the professions' legal framework and its practical realities was such that an overhaul was imperative. In certain big cities, 20 per cent of dispensaries were not actually managed by a pharmacist as required by the Germinal law. 'The cause of the problems and contradictions the profession was struggling with was essentially the economic and technical development that had confronted the new forms of pharmaceutical capitalism with traditional methods of production and sale'.[32] The leaders of the profession tried to establish a common position and put forward concrete proposals for reform, based on the idea of self-organisation by the profession. But the mistrust and rivalry between the two warring sectors were a strong delaying factor in the long overdue reform of the legislation.

The corporatist and authoritarian Vichy regime passed the law of 11 September 1941 which dissolved the unions, groups and professional bodies representing the interests of the pharmaceutical profession.[33] Paul Métadier commented:

> The reforms I had recommended could only work effectively through the value of the professional organisation that would implement them. But the new bodies representing the pharmaceutical profession were placed under the external authority of the State ... It was a great disappointment. We did not obtain the Order and we lost the unions.

However, this law did contain a significant innovation: establishments that prepared or sold simple drugs or chemical products in bulk for

pharmacy could belong to a limited liability company, on condition that
the chairman and half plus one of the board members were pharmacists.
Intended as a liberalising law, it in fact accelerated the pharmaceutical
industry's adoption of a characteristic dual structure, where one company
would simply own trademarks and would not be subject to this obligation,
while the second company would manufacture the products and would
comply with it in terms of management composition. L'Équilibre Biologique
and Laboratoires Joullié functioned in this way from the start. Robert &
Carrière created their own development company after the war. The law
also instituted a Minister of Health marketing authorisation for brand
medicines, which was granted 'when it presents a character of novelty and
a therapeutic advantage, and offers no danger to the moral and physical
health of the population'. Possession of this authorisation bestowed 'a
guarantee against imitation for a period of six years'.[34]

The new law was thus revolutionary in several regards: it made the
exploitation of a medicine, existing or planned, subject to the approval
of the public authorities, following a technical evaluation and an assessment of the product's therapeutic value. Previously, brand medicines had
simply been registered by the National Drug Inspection Laboratory, so
that they would obtain the certificates sometimes required for export
purposes and appear on the list of products reimbursed by the social
security system, although this reimbursement was not imposed by any
legal requirement. This increased regulation was accompanied by a considerable advantage, the appearance of a form of protection whereby the
State granted a monopoly of exploitation of new drugs for a period of
six years.

The gradual reintegration of pharmaceutical innovation into common
law had begun, but it had a long way to go still, notwithstanding the
eloquence of its advocates. Paul Métadier wrote:

> The proprietary drug is an invention that simply lacks a patent ... The
> pharmacist must have the possibility of becoming an inventor, either by his
> natural ingenuity, or by scientific research. The notion of the invention helps
> maintain the prestige of our profession ... A new product, unless it has been
> proved harmful, should not be treated as an unlawful product.[35]

Resistance by the dispensaries to the industrialization of drug manufacture
was now becoming a rearguard action. Pharmacists were understanding at
long last that:

> the proprietary medicine is not an enemy. It can become a valuable ally. It
> has created business levels much higher than with magistral preparations.
> Proprietary medicine producers have moved pharmacy onto a scale that it
> would never have reached with the necessarily restricted resources of the
> dispensary. In 1931, the turnover of the pharmaceutical firms was assessed

at 1,200 million on the domestic market alone. These revenues, in excess of one billion, have not been taken from retailers, but given to them. The growth of the proprietary medicine has benefited pharmacists ... The more such products there are, the better the pharmacists will do. Specialisation in everything, everywhere, is the modern form of contemporary business.[36]

After the war, a National Order of Pharmacists was instituted on 5 May 1945, with the aim of ensuring 'the respect for professional duties, the defence of the honour and independence of the profession'. It enshrined in law the profession's desire to organise itself. Nonetheless, its autonomy remained restricted by the new legislative framework, and the industry retained its peculiar twin-company structure.

The 1941 law solved some of the problems that were a legacy of the Germinal law, but left some of the most pressing ones unaddressed. A measure of reconciliation was making its way between the enemy brothers, the pharmacists and the industrialists, but the financing of the pharmaceutical firms was still hampered by restrictions that reflected the reluctance of the authorities to consider their activities as fully industrial in nature and as much in need of investment as any other sector.

In the 'thirty glorious years' of expansion that followed the Second World War, the French pharmaceutical industry grew very fast, with drug consumption growing twice as quickly as that of other products. Faced with this tremendous explosion in needs, the industry concentrated on priorities. Entangled in an administrative morass which limited its investment capacities, but still confronted by the necessity of bringing to French markets revolutionary new products like the sulfamides, antibiotics and corticoids, it began a renewal of the pharmacopoeia. The 1950s saw the launch of multiple combinations of known active principles. Over the next decade, many new foreign products were taken under licence while the foundations of autonomous research in synthetic chemistry were laid. But the priority was production, with the need to distribute medicines which had become accessible to the French people through improvements in standards of living and the creation of the Social Security system by the orders of 4 October 1945, which organised the collective financing of health spending.

The industry's structural problems remained fundamental. Drug manufacture had attained such a scale that questions were beginning to be asked about the need for it to remain a monopoly of pharmacists, and about the value of the 1941 law requiring the latter to be majority shareholders and board members in pharmaceutical firms. At the same time, the profession was politically weakened by attacks on it arising out of the expansion of the Social Security budget, as the categories of the population covered were extended. Drug prices were set by the government, under the much disputed price regulations, which was not without its perverse effects.

Moreover, prices were subject to repeated unilateral reductions and lagged well behind inflation. The horizontal concentration of structures, the vertical integration of activities, from the manufacture of raw materials to commercialisation, and the intensification of promotion to doctors, were all methods introduced to counter these problems.

The first hesitant steps were taken to shift research from outside pharmaceutical firms to within them. For a long time, their role had been to fund projects or external researchers who were closely linked to them by contract. Gradually, the more dynamic companies, those that would manage the move to a larger scale, equipped themselves with their own autonomous research centres, The Robert & Carrière board was to note in 1966:

> Research in the pharmaceutical industry has become more difficult in recent years. The discovery of original active principles has become increasingly lengthy, costly and chancy. In synthetic chemistry, which is one of our main activities, once the simplest molecules have been studied and made, we need to move towards increasingly complicated structures, which require lengthy research. In addition, as pharmaceutical firms throughout the world employ growing numbers of ever more specialised researchers, improved techniques and more extensive material resources, research in the pharmaceutical industry is becoming a matter of intense international competition. Moreover, the concern for public health protection has led to a rise in experimentation and in clinical testing. In consequence, many years may elapse between the discovery of a new active principle and its becoming available to the medical community as a proprietary medicine. Research in the pharmaceutical industry is in fact the equivalent of a medium term investment.

International competition also affected the commercialisation of new products, as explained by the same board minute:

> Every day, it is becoming more difficult for French pharmaceutical firms to acquire rights to exploit new foreign drugs. American firms in particular prefer to entrust the exploitation of their new products to their (French) subsidiaries, or else offer them to firms that have their own research functions and can provide them with other products in return.

For all these reasons, including government incentives for research and concentration, French pharmaceutical firms were faced by the necessity to invest massively in scientific research and to increase production capacity. Some resigned themselves to take-over by foreign companies, others chose to go down the road of concentration by combining their investment capacities with those of other similar sized firms.

Changes in structures

The order of 23 May 1945, which completed the law of 11 September 1941 on the capital structure of pharmaceutical firms, required in principle that the majority of the equity of these companies, whatever their form, must belong either to one or more pharmacists registered with the Pharmaceutical Council, or to the State. Nationalization was the order of the day, and had affected whole swathes of the economy. The threat was clear. A long battle began, which would end with the opening of pharmaceutical firms' capital to non-pharmacist shareholders in 1955.

The 1941 law was meant to have a liberalising effect. Under the 135 year old Germinal law, only qualified pharmacists could own a pharmacy. Any establishment that made medicines was considered to be covered by this provision, as the law obviously could not foresee the industrial manufacture of medicines. As this required capital like any other industrial process, it had developed in a legal vacuum which, in reality, tolerated all kinds of arrangements. The 1945 order, under the pretence of enacting a more liberal law and of bringing outmoded legislation up to date, actually sought to restore order to the industry and to maintain the principle of the full and complete responsibility of health professionals in drug manufacture, by using the threat of state ownership to force the industry to restructure in accordance with this principle.

Robert & Carrière was directly targeted by this measure which posed it 'almost inextricable practical difficulties'.[37] For reasons that went back to the company's industrial origins, most of its equity did not belong to qualified pharmacists. Under these circumstances, the directors proved above all keen to avoid state participation. But this was not the only possible outcome to be feared. The consequence of applying the 1945 order would have been to change the composition of the share structure and of the board of directors, which would in turn have entailed changes in the management team. It was also contrary to the articles of the company which stipulated that the transfer of shares to anyone other than an existing shareholder had to be approved by the board. In addition, it could affect capital increases, which would have to give priority to pharmacist shareholders.

The event was to cause a triple crisis: first a conflict between the shareholders who disagreed on the measures to take, then a mobilisation of the profession, which filed an appeal with the Minister of Health. Finally, it led to structural changes which were to outlive the imperatives that had made them necessary.

The initial reaction of the management was to create in 1946, 'as a precaution and to cover any eventuality',[38] a Laboratoires Robert & Carrière operating company which would exploit the business as a going concern belonging to the laboratories. It was an SARL (private limited company) with a share ownership and board structure as laid down by the law, so as to 'allow Laboratoires Robert & Carrière, which would grant it a manufacturing and sales licence, to conform to the provisions of the order, while avoiding state participation'.[39] The SARL was 40 per cent owned by Laboratoires Robert & Carrière, 50.2 percent by pharmacists. The research laboratory remained the property of the SA (public limited liability company), together with the new products and the brands. As a strict separation of the research and production activities had to be observed, the SARL had to remain an operating company which returned its profits to the SA in the form of royalties.

The reaction of the non-pharmacist shareholders, who felt themselves threatened with having to transfer or reduce their holdings in the company, was not slow to come, and was a measure of their attachment to the firm. They created an Association of non-pharmacist shareholders and went to the Service central de la pharmacie (administrative body in charge of pharmacy) to 'express their grievances and ask for special consideration of (their) company's position'.[40] In April 1947, two hundred pharmaceutical firms signed a petition to the Health Minister asking for at least a postponement of the order's application date.

The return to what the profession recognised to have been the pre-war 'freedom of capital' was the outcry, which was significant of the state of anarchy that the gradual fading out of the Germinal law had entailed. It took place in several stages. In June 1947, 'the Health Minister seem(ed) to have given up state ownership of pharmaceutical firms'.[41] A few months later, a bill was introduced to modify the 1945 order, which met with hostility from the Health Ministry but was well received by the Ministries of Finance and of Industrial Production. 'The pharmaceutical industry', declared Mr. Prevet, 'has been unable, since the application of the said order, to find the capital essential to it'.[42] The banks let it be known that they would refuse to lend to pharmaceutical firm operating companies. Even the order's contents were ambiguous, since the description of its purpose stated that 'a wide debate needs to be opened on the changes, from which the government will ensure that it draws the maximum advantage for the establishment of the final Pharmacy charter'. Under the circumstances, the order was viewed as 'a provisional text which would never be applied and which was simply intended as guidance for the writers of a definitive law'.[43] In the absence of any prior discussion, there was full latitude for debate after the publication of the order, which was not followed by any decree of application. A general wait-and-see policy was the rule in the profession.

But five years later, the decree of 20 May 1955 restored freedom of capital ownership in the pharmaceutical industry for companies with equity in excess of 50 million francs. In this way, the industry's growth requirements were at last recognised and its trend towards concentration implicitly encouraged. Indeed, the profession was far from unanimous on the subject. Opposition to the decree grew within several professional pharmacy bodies. The National Order of Pharmacists in particular appealed to the Council of State. In practice, the existence of an operating company structure probably appeared to afford more advantages than disadvantages.

The launching of the process of concentration

If the question of letting the pharmaceutical industry have access to the sources of financing it needed raised so much debate, concentration of the industry was strongly encouraged. The restructuring of the French pharmaceutical industry during the years of post-war economic growth was indeed spectacular. Of the two thousand pharmaceutical firms that existed at the Liberation, of which a good half were simply dispensary annexes, there remained in 1964 'seven hundred provisional survivors'.[44] In 1970, only 450 remained, in other words one in ten of the original dispensary annexes, and one industrial pharmaceutical firm in two. The number of drug manufacturers fell by almost 40 per cent in the space of a few years. In terms of market share, concentration was even more rapid. In 1958, 43 firms accounted for two-thirds of the industry's turnover. 15 years later, the 50 biggest companies shared 80 per cent.

A significant process of bunching between medium-sized family firms was taking place. In 1964, the financial paper *Les Échos* prided itself on publishing for the first time, in an era when economic information was far from what it is today,[46] a ranking of the top fifty pharmaceutical firms according to their 1961 turnover. All the future companies of the Synthélabo Group were there. The turnovers of the group's future companies lay in a range between twelve million francs and 63 million francs in 1961. The three market leaders of the time, Spécia, the pharmaceutical branch of the Rhône-Poulenc group, Roussel-Uclaf and Clin-Byla, had respective turnovers of 250 million francs, 200 million francs and 145 million francs.

For those medium-sized pharmaceutical firms that survived the increasing burden of regulation and managed, thanks to a few good products, to stay in control of the expansion process and to keep up with the industrialisation of pharmaceutical production, the alliance between businesses of similar size was a winning strategy, in terms of cost rationalisation and the pooling of resources for research. The alternative was to go down with all hands as had so many competitors or to 'sell the business as a going concern to the Americans'[46] who, with the advance they had gained from the major public investment in medical research during the war, were seeking to gain a foothold in Europe to extend their markets. Direct imports of drugs were tightly regulated, but the acquisition of firms with existing facilities and sales networks enabled competing foreign firms to get around the problem by manufacturing and packaging locally, using imported active principles.

The contraction of this web of craft-based pharmaceutical firms, most of which were born of the success of an over-the-counter product launched in the dispensary, had multiple causes. Many of the products they had were old indeed, but they were proven and still enjoyed a good reputation. However, tightly bound as they had been since 1948 by the freeze in prices, which made French medicines the cheapest in Europe, these firms became less profitable. They did not have the resources to find ways round the freeze, as did the bigger players who invested in combinations of existing active principles with which they could obtain new approvals and hence prices calculated according to the new standards, however artificial, of the price regulations. In this totally controlled market, launching products that were either genuinely or supposedly new was a technical necessity, as much an effect of price regulation as a commercial imperative of survival in the face of competition. The pharmaceutical firms for whom the balance of power with their foreign partners was more favourable began on a policy of co-operation and licence acquisition which enabled innovative drugs developed during the war, notably penicillin, to enter the French market.

The Malthusian policy of restricting the entry of non-pharmaceutical new capital into the industry had been a considerable brake on investment for a long time. Likewise, the 1941 law introducing administrative approval for drugs left small firms in a difficult position. The formalities for establishing the technical documentation were burdensome, expensive and often beyond the reach of companies with limited resources, even supposing that the therapeutic value of their products was sufficient to obtain approval. Yet approval was commercially essential, as it was a condition of Social Security reimbursement.

The profound reform of the regulations introduced by the order of 4 February 1959 gave a boost to the concentration process. By making subcontracting more difficult, by accentuating technical controls, i.e., by imposing de facto investment in personnel and equipment which was beyond their reach, it made the survival of the smaller firms problematical. But above all, it made drugs patentable at long last, which discouraged copies – the salvation of innovation-starved companies – in favour of efforts in research that were increasingly costly but indispensable to therapeutic progress.[47] It thus gave the industry the impetus it needed to turn to modern methods of research and to compete in an industry which was becoming increasingly international in scope.

NOTES

1. 21 germinal, year XI of the French revolutionary calendar (12 April 1803).
2. Several of the case studies referred to in this paper (Laboratoires Dausse et Robert & Carrière, Métabio-Joullié) are among the five founding firms of the French group Synthélabo, created in 1970, which merged with Sanofi in 1999 to form the new group Sanofi-Synthélabo. See M. Ruffat, *175 years of the French Pharmaceutical Industry, A History of Synthélabo* (Paris, La Découverte, 1998).
3. *Pharmacia*, 20 March 1910, quoted by Viviane Thévenin, 'The School and the Dispensary, Pharmacists from 1871 to 1919', in Claire Salomon-Bayet, *Pasteur et la révolution pastorienne* (Payot, 1986), p. 188.
4. Émile de la Bédollière, 'Le pharmacien', Curver, *Les Français par eux-mêmes*, 1842.
5. *La Pharmacie coopérative*, March 1903.
6. Les Laboratoires Dausse is the oldest of the laboratories that were to form the Synthélabo group. Amans Dauss launched his dispensary in 1834.
7. Memorandum dated 9 May 1933.
8. 'General Laboratory for Sterilisation by the Robert & Carrière processes'. Mr. Carrière was a wax and candle maker. Wax was a product of common use in pharmacy, and its sterilising properties at high temperature were well known.
9. Register of companies no. 81814, Archives of the Tribunal de Commerce.
10. Robert & Carrière annual shareholders' meeting, 29 April 1931.
11. Maître Marcel Plaisant, *La Loi*, 18 January 1936. When the brand name was simply a reference to the chemical composition of the product, so to speak a repetition of the formula, the courts refused to recognise such names as brand names. Hence the proliferation of Greek and Latin names, a late acknowledgement of the origins and the perennial use of ancient languages in medicine and pharmacy.
12. François Prevet, *Essai sur l'exercice de la pharmacie appliquée à l'industrie pharmaceutique*, (Sirey, 1937), p. 16.
13. Ibid., p. 17.
14. Robert & Carrière annual shareholders' meeting, 14 June 1934.
15. Prevet, *Essai sur l'exercice de la pharmacie*, p. 20.
16. Armand Valeur, *Rapport sur l'industrie pharmaceutique*, Turin International Exhibition of Industry and Labour, 1911, p. 67.
17. Paul Métadier, *La Pharmacie en 1945*, Les Laboratoires Métadier, 1945, p. 23.
18. William Breckon, *The Drug Makers*, (London, 1972), p. 13.
19. Alexandre Blondeau, *Histoire des laboratoires pharmaceutiques en France*, Paris, Le Cherche-Midi, 1992, p. 15.
20. Métadier, *La Pharmacie en 1945*.
21. The law of 5 July 1844, article 3, declared all kinds of remedies unpatentable.
22. For fear that the confusion between the generic term and the trademark should lead to a monopoly on the product. This rule was circumvented by the use of 'fancy' names.

23. Prevet, *Essai sur l'exercice de la pharmacie*, p. 18.
24. The Revolution of 1789 had introduced the principle of industrial property. Contrary to the commonly held view at the time that ideas were immaterial and the shared property of humanity, the law enacted on 7 January 1791, (relating to useful discoveries and to the means of ensuring their ownership to those recognised as being their authors) acknowledged that intellectual creation must be protected from plagiarism. In the absence of patents applicable to medicines, it was this notion of intellectual property that inventors of medicines would use to uphold their rights.
25. Robert & Carrière annual shareholders' meeting of 4 June 1927.
26. The bacteriophage is a virus which parasitises bacteria and destroys them through lysis. In Professor d'Hérelle's own terms, it acts 'like an infectious illness which attacks bacteria'. Bacteriophages were thus used therapeutically to fight the bacteria specific to several diseases, like colibacillus, the typhus bacillus, the dysentery bacillus or staphylococcus.
27. Robert & Carrière annual shareholders' meeting, 22 May 1926.
28. Robert & Carrière annual shareholders' meeting, 30 December 1922.
29. Métadier, *La Pharmacie en 1938*, p. 5.
30. At the same time as managing his company, Paul Métadier, a powerful personality, won an audience in the profession and became one of its spokesmen. By distributing the *Lettre pharmaceutique* (Pharmaceutical Letter), he publicised his ideas on the its evolution and the legislative reforms he believed necessary. In particular, on the eve of the war he was pressing for the creation of an Order of Pharmacists, based on the idea that 'when a profession is organised, it makes the laws. As our profession is not organised, others make them for us'.
31. Métadier, *La Pharmacie en 1945*, p. 17.
32. Ibid., p.22
33. Robert & Carrierè Article 60 of the law of 11 September 1941.
34. Robert & Carrierè Article 44 of the law of 11 September 1941.
35. Métadier, *La Pharmacie en 1938*, p. 20.
36. Ibid., p. 21.
37. Robert & Carrière Board meeting of 14 April 1947.
38. Annual shareholders' meeting of 30 June 1950.
39. Board meeting of 14 April 1947.
40. Robert & Carrière annual shareholders' meeting of 30 June 1950.
41. Robert & Carrière Board meeting of 27 June 1947.
42. Robert & Carrière Board meeting of 1 May 1948.
43. Robert & Carrière annual shareholders' meeting of 16 May 1947.
44. 'The strange worlds of the drug. III. The late French pharmaceutical industry?', *Le Monde*, 30 January 1965.
45. The great majority of pharmaceutical firms were not stock market quoted and did not therefore need to publish their results.
46. *Le Monde*, 30 January 1965.
47. Jacqueline Sigvard, *L'Industrie du médicament* (Paris, 1975), p. 43–4.

Between Merchants and Criminals: the System of Values of Soviet Entrepreneurs in the 1920s Under the New Economic Policy

Serguey Cheikhetov

Central European University

In this paper I am going to discuss the system of values of the Soviet private entrepreneurs. This social group included both urban traders and manufacturers, who were engaged in business during a short period of Soviet history - the period of New Economical Policy [NEP]. Despite the apparent interest of scholars in the problems concerning NEP and nepmen, one important aspect of the history of the 'Last Russian Capitalists' as Alan A. Ball calls them, has escaped the attention of historians.[1] This aspect is the nepmen's system of values.

First of all it is necessary to determine the notion of 'system of values'. For me the system of values is one of the main characteristics of every social group. A developed system of values is a sign of the independence of a social group, its isolation from the influence of other social strata. It is also a sign of the fact that members of this group realise such categories as 'we' and 'they'. The presence or absence of the system of values character-ises the extent of the maturity and stability of social links between the members of a group. The system of values regulates the behaviour of members of the group in different situations and determines their tastes, life styles and moral qualities.

It is extremely difficult to reconstruct the whole system of values of the Soviet entrepreneurs because of a shortage of sources. Entrepreneurs in the Soviet Union as well as in other countries aspired to keep their private lives to themselves. But the sources do allow us to reconstruct the main elements which represent a basic part of the nepmen's system of values.[2] These elements include their attitudes towards wealth, labour, the power of the state and finally their attitude towards everyday life or lifestyle. This paper seeks to explore the aforementioned elements of the nepmen's sys-tem of values and compare them with the pre-Revolutionary Russian merchants' system of values. It is my intention to prove that the nepmen inherited many values from pre-revolutionary merchants, but that during the 1920s the values of the old Russian bourgeoisie were replaced by the values of the criminal world. I also intend to show how the nepmen's values influenced other social groups of Soviet society and to try to evaluate this influence.

Before giving an analysis of the nepmen's system of values it is necessary to describe briefly NEP and nepmen within the historical context. The period of NEP began in March 1921 when the Tenth Party Congress proclaimed NEP and abolished restrictions on private business. Immediately after that a huge number of people turned to private trade and later to private industry. This new social group was extremely mixed. Only a few of the new entrepreneurs had been engaged in commerce prior to the Revolution. The majority of them were workers, peasants, soldiers, civil servants and artisans who had little or no experience in this field.

These private entrepreneurs, or nepmen, had a very definite legal status; they were deprived of all civic rights. This meant that they could not vote or engage in civic services, and had to pay additional taxes, etc. Although, at the same time nepmen enjoyed a higher standard of living than many other groups within the population. Therefore their social position was characterised by a duality: from one perspective they were at the bottom of the social hierarchy, from another they could reach the top of it.

The state policy towards nepmen ranged between degrees of tolerance, but was usually characterised by hostility. The Soviet state needed nepmen to restore the destroyed economy, but at the same time it was frightened of nepmen as potential counterrevolutionaries. That is why the handling of private capital was set within rigid limits. Nepmen had no right to engage in foreign trade and in many branches of industry. In addition, they had to pay a mass of extra taxes and work in a hostile environment. So, the conditions of private entrepreneurship in the Soviet Union in the 1920s were very hard. Nepmen had to hide their operations and permanently cheat the state to survive. At the end of the 1920s Bolsheviks moved from a policy of 'hostile tolerance' to the liquidation of private capital. By a variety of methods, government drove nepmen out of the economy. Some ex-nepmen continued their business illegally, but we cannot consider them private entrepreneurs in the true sense as they merged with the criminal world and lost their group's identitiy.[3] So the short history of Soviet private entrepreneurs concludes at the beginning of the 1930s.

The hard conditions under which nepmen had to work accelerated the formation of the nepmen's system of values. At the beginning of the 1920s the nepmen already appreciated their common interests and consciously opposed the external social environment. One can often find in the nepmen's correspondence the combination of words 'alien elements' (*chuzdie elementi*).[4] The nepmen applied this epithet to the representatives of bureaucracy and less frequently to the workers. The Soviet private entrepreneurs sought to isolate themselves from other social groups. This aspiration manifested itself in the manner of dressing, in the lifestyles and idiosyncransies of behaviour. Moreover the nepmen wanted to isolate not only themselves, but also their children. One can find eloquent evidence of this in the numerous but vain attempts of the nepmen to organise their own schools. In 1925, the committee of the private entrepreneurs of Novosibirsk initiated a project to create elementary and secondary schools. The authors of the project intended to reserve 75 per cent of places for nepmen's children and make only 25 per cent available to others. Remarkably, some entrepreneurs were against giving even a single place to workers and peasants.[5] This surely contradicts the widespread theory that nepmen sensed the end of NEP and feared for the vulnerability of their social positions?[6] Had they had such a sense, their actions would indicate that they were interested in the present day only and were not concerned about the future. For, if private entrepreneurs understood that the future looked bleak surely they would have tried to incorporate their children into the other social groups.

The formation of the nepmen as an independent social group was indissolubly linked with the emergence of their system of values. One of the main elements of this system was an aspiration to wealth. The newspapers of the 1920s are full of feuilletons about nepmen who would do everything for the purpose of enrichment. The anecdote about nepman Pugovkin, who did not hesitate to get rich at the expense of other people's misfortunes, distinctively characterises this nepman feature. Small trader Pugovkin read about a major earthquake in Japan in 1923 and was very happy because he just bought a batch of Japanese tools. Pugovkin was going to raise the price and sell these tools but on a second thought he decided to wait and see if there was going to be another earthquake in Japan. If that happened, he could raise the prices higher still.[7]

The anecdote about Pugovkin is only anecdote, although it clearly reflects the nepmen's desire for wealth. Here is a real story which occurred in Siberia at the beginning of NEP. The currency speculators from the so-called 'black market' (*chernay ploshadka*) made the price of the tsarist ten-ruble piece jump from 52 million soviet rubles to 80 million within three days. As a result, all goods sharply rose in price. The participants of this shady transaction did not escape punishment. Sixty malicious speculators were arrested.[8]

As swindling among private entrepreneurs became increasingly common place, so words were found to classify the different types of swindlers that emerged. For example, the second-hand dealers who used various tricks to make the peasants sell them grain for a very low price, got the nicknames 'marmosets' (*martishki*) and 'drivers, persons who pen or drive cattle' (*zagonyli*).[9] The speculators who operated in furs were called 'suitcasers' (*chemodanshiki*)[10], thanks to the huge suitcases in which they transported their commodities. The nepmen who borrowed credits from state organisations and did not return money were called 'cat skinners'(*koshkodrali*).[11] Very often the nepmen came close to bankruptcy. Sometimes the creation of private enterprise had only one purpose – to achieve bankruptcy. This sort of enterprise was given a special name – 'Grievous company' (*Coreko*).

Cases of swindling involving private enterpreneurs and state or cooperative organizations were numerous. The case of the private association 'Toiler' (*Truzinnik*) provides a typical example. The owners of *Truzennik*, nepmen well known in Siberia like Lisizin, Kookarzev, Vagin and Sorokin, enriched themselves at the expense of the cooperative organization 'SOZ'. Having bribed the manager of 'SOZ', they managed to get deficient goods through the cooperative and pay only a nominal price for them. The cooperation between the private entrepreneurs and the corrupt manager lasted from 1923 to 1925. As a result the association 'SOZ' reached bankruptcy.[12]

The aspiration for enrichment determined the nepmen's attitude towards labour. Nepmen considered business the major and most important part of life. Everything outside business was considered secondary. Nepmen worked extremely hard, not taking vacations, working at weekends and during the night. They regularly travelled huge distances in pursuit of business. Nepmen often suffered hardships and some starved.[13] They not only exhausted themselves but also made their employees work hard. There was no notion of the 'length of working day' in these private enterprises. The work was not over until it was fully completed. However, nepmen were rarely the heartless exploiters that Soviet propaganda continually painted them to be. Consideration for the welfare of employees was considered fundamental to the success of a business.

Sometimes entrepreneurs dealt with non-profitable business in the interests of their employees. For example, the tenant of a gold mine, Pavlov appreciated that his enterprise was unprofitable. It was in his interests to nullify the contract. But Pavlov did not want to deprive his employees, who were old and loyal, of a piece of bread. That is why Pavlov continued his business two years more.[14] Another example, the tenant of salt-mines Byiski, was well known in Siberia not only because of his enterprising activity, but also because of his care he displayed towards his employees. Byiski built new houses for workers, a worker's club, library, chemist and gym. To be fair, Byiski was an exception. Usually nepmen economised on the social aspects of their employees' lives.[15]

The nepmens' attitude towards state power was an important component of their system of values. To some extent, it is this that determined the formation of the nepmen as a social group. Nepmen disliked Soviet power but tried to tolerate it. The nepmen's demands of the state were not highly principled in character and did not encroach upon the basis of the state policy towards private capital. But one issue was an exception – the deprivation of their electoral rights. Nepmen did not want to resign themselves to their low social status and repeatedly protested against the law. For example, the owner of a large shop in Novosibirsk, Boohalov told the journalist of the Siberian regional newspaper 'Soviet Siberia' (Sovetskay Sibir): 'Why have they deprived me of my rights? I pay more taxes than others. ... Soviet power deprives me of a voice, it keeps me silent. Liberal Russia must not have stepsons. But in fact we are the stepsons'.[16] Remarkably, Boohalov stresses simultaneously both democratic values (Liberal Russia must not have stepsons) and his exceptional status in the society (I pay more taxes than others). This dual-consciousness was common among nepmen.

The political activity of nepmen was limited to declarations and never evolved into active forms of struggle against the Soviet regime. Even OGPU[17], which saw counterrevolution everywhere, had to admit this fact.[18] Generally speaking, the nepmen's attitude towards Soviet power can be described as patient obedience. Private entrepreneurs hoped that the state would, sooner or later realise the usefulness of private capital and change its policy towards nepmen. However this did not prevent nepmen from cheating the state as often as possible.

The nepmen's attitude towards the state changed during NEP. At the beginning and even in the mid-1920s, nepmen enthusiastically supported all decrees directed at stimulating private business. In 1924, the government issued a decree about privileges for the private gold industry, and nepmen immediately moved their capital to this sector.[19] But only four years later in 1928 nepmen practically ignored an analogous decree concerning privileges for the private construction industry.[20] Having experienced how the state could deceive them, nepmen supposed that it was another way to coax their money from them. So nepmen gradually lost their confidence in the Soviet authorities.

Attitudes towards wealth and labour determined the nepmen's lifestyles. Nepmen had to own their house, servants, and dress smartly to be respected in the business world. Nepmen paid great attention to their clothing. Clothing enabled nepmen to distinguish themselves from representatives of other social groups. An English suit, a silk shirt, polished shoes and walking-stick were indispensable attributes of the dress of an average manufacturer or trader. In winter, nepmen dressed in expensive fur-coats. This 'uniform' was common among nepmen from Moscow and Leningrad as well as among nepmen from remote provinces. There were also definite rules for women's dress. Nepmen's wives wore narrow, back-lengthened, expensive – silk, brocade and fur – dresses, creating the 'bird silhouette'. The likeness to a bird was increased by a short haircut and a small cap closely fitted to the head and sometimes pulled over one eye. Narrow pointed shoes completed this costume. Nepmen, both men and women, aspired to emphasise a high price and luxury of their dress. The dress showed the status of a person in the business world.[21]

According to the nepmen's system of values, a particular vice was stinginess. Nepmen had to be seen to waste money to earn of the respect of their colleagues. One contemporary wrote of their business customs

> In 1922 a certain Abram Abramovich from Moscow bought sables in Yriankhay krai [Southern Siberia] and on the Usa river. He decided to make a party for his colleagues to brag about his Moscow boldness. At the height of the party, the 'amiable' host organised a cards game for the 'amiable' guests. Initially they bet on money, then passed to furs. The excited, drunken players shouted, stimulating each other
> –bet 10 sables
> –repeat 15
> –I am not frightened by you – bet 25
> At this moment, the excited Abram Abramovich suddenly dealt on the table a heavy blow with his fist and loudly shouted to his employee: 'Monka, bring the sack with sables here. I will show these shy Siberian fellows how the Moscovites play!' Monka brought the sack following the order of his master, and Abram Abramovich, with the triumphant look of a winner, took out several hundred sables on the table. 'Bet all these sables' – shouted the intoxicated master. The effect was very strong Even Siberian speculators who bought and sold hundreds and thousands of precious furs were shocked.[22]

The nepmen in remote provinces and nepmen in the capital shared a desire for luxurious lifestyles and gambling. A Frenchman in Moscow at the beginning of the 1920s made the following observations

> Banks at baccarat frequently ran as high as 5,000 dollars, a dozen different currencies were used, from bundles of Soviet million notes to hundred-dollar bills, English five- and ten-pound notes, and most surprising of all, no small quantity of gold, Tsarist ten-rouble pieces, English sovereigns and French twenty-franc coins. The biggest gambling establishment was a place called Praga at the corner of the Arbat Square. In the main outer room there were two roulette tables both with zero and double zero, two baccarat tables and a dozen games of *chemin de fer*. As in France, there was an inner '*cercle privé*', where only baccarat was allowed and play was higher, with banks of 25,000 and 30,000 dollars.[23]

The family life of the private entrepreneurs was also regulated by unwritten rules. Nepmen had to marry to earn respect among their fellow entrepreneurs. Marriage was a sign of trustworthiness and seriousness of a person. Besides, the nepmen's wife played an important role in commerce. Wives assisted their husbands in business and headed the enterprise after the husband's death or arrest (this happened rather often).

Nepmen endeavoured to keep their private life secret, to protect their reputation in the business world. Trying to do so, they sometimes infringed the law. For example, the trial of the nepman Petr Ivanov provoked great indignation in the press. Ivanov had to marry. The interests of the business required it. But Ivanov had been infected by syphilis for many years. Having said no word about the disease to his wife, Ivanov married. As a result Ivanov's wife, their baby and the wet nurse were also infected.[24]

Nepmen respected family, but did not uphold marital faithfulness. On the contrary, their lifestyles, though considered by the majority to be dissolute and deprived, were considered standard among entrepreneurs. That was the reason why nepmen often spent their free time in different dens. In these dens the entrepreneurs could relax and rest in a pleasant environment. They also made acquaintance with useful people there, and discussed details of the business.

Nepmen also considered it decent to visit theatres during free time. However the theatrical tastes of nepmen were rather simplistic. These are the words of an indignant critic 'Today they want "Night of love", tomorrow – sentimental melodrama or something about the Tsars Romanov's life, after tomorrow – farce with striptease or stupid comedy'.[25] The repertoire of the Theatre 'Intimate' (*Intimniy*) in Novonikolaevsk, which was considered 'nepmenish', included the following 'My mother in law is pregnant', 'The carriage of daddies and one mother', 'The old men and girls', the titles speak for themselves.[26]

To an overwhelming extent, advertising was targeted at the nepmen. This advertising indicates that a further entertainment, in addition to the dens and the theatre,[27] was popular among the nepmen: it was the so-called 'educational shows'. The educational level of these shows was very low. For example, the lectures of a certain Nikolay Luganski who toured the province in 1927 were a great success. This lecturer pretended to be a professor of Moscow Theatrical University, which never actually existed, and held a lecture entitled 'The spiritual essence of the female's body'. The advertisement for this 'educational' show promised: 'The lecture will be accompanied by the strong ballet of the incomparable Cleo Lugansli, and after that debate will take place'.[28]

This all shows that the nepmen's system of values had many features in common with the system of values of pre-Revolutionary Russian merchants. Both of these social groups were similar in their attitudes towards wealth, labour, state power, family, etc. It would be logical to assume that nepmen borrowed much from representatives of the ex-merchants estate.[29] Remarkably, only ten per cent of the social group of nepmen were ex-merchants, but they could force the representatives of the other social groups (workers, peasants, officers, etc.) to accept their values.[30]

Despite obvious similarities between nepmens' and pre-Revolutionary merchants' systems of values, there were also essential differences. For example merchants did not consider the deception of the consumer as a sin, but according to their system of values it was absolutely forbidden to deceive their colleagues. The merchant's word of honour was considered sacred. For nepmen, the word of honour lost its significance. They kept their promises only if it was profitable for them. Nepmen were prepared to be quite ruthless, for example to denounce their colleagues to OGPU to get rid of competitors. For instance, a trader from Krasnoyrsk Zolbershteyn desperate for the authorities' favour often informed OGPU how his competitors were going to hide their valuables.[31] The pre-Revolutionary merchants infringed the law but, nevertheless, they had definite moral restrictions and never transgressed them. Nepmen had no such inhibitions. In the 1920s swindlers ruled among nepmen. The unfair business was considered normal and even valiant. Neither were nepmen afraid to undertake 'dirty' businesses such as drug-dealing, buying-up of stolen goods, keeping of dens, etc.[32] The emergence of these values is a sign that the criminal world impacted upon nepmen. The impetuous development of the so-called 'black economics' during the 1920s gives us grounds to judge that the influence of the criminal world became dominant at the end of the 1920s and the criminal values usurped other values in the nepmens' consciousness.

We cannot complete the analysis of the nepmens' system of values without analyzing its impact on other social groups within Soviet society. This impact was very considerable. It is quite remarkable that all attempts of the authorities to indoctrinate nepmen in the communist belief failed. Neither the persuasive methods of the trade unions nor administrative measures could make nepmen change their minds. At the same time nepmen very successfully affected other social groups. Their values, particularly aspiration to enrichment and aspiration to a comfortable life, infiltrated the consciousness of the Soviet people. Even communists and representatives of the intelligentsia who seemed far from entrepreneurship, could not escape nepmen's influence. In 1926, newspapers discussed intently the trial of Chanribsouz. This big private enterprise was masked as the fishermen's cooperative. The inspirer and organiser of this enterprise was a certain Gornunk – a young fellow, who graduated from the History and Philosophy departments of Moscow State University. Razumovski, a member of the Communist Party and Suchanov and Kochedamov, nepmen, well known in Siberia maintained Chanribsouz together with Gornunk.[33] The nepmen's lifestyles, their manner of behaviour attracted people. As the head of Siberian regional court angrily wrote in his circular, '... the majority of judges and milicioners (police officers) preferred nepmen to members of party to have as friends. So they fell under the nepmen's influence'.[34]

Nepmen were the legislators of fashion. Music-halls and theatres orientated towards the nepmen's tastes. The representatives of other social groups aspired to imitate nepmen's lifestyle. The professional jargon of nepmen rapidly spread among population and became part of colloquial language.[35] All these facts are evidence of the great influence of the nepmen's values.

To sum up, one can conclude that nepmen had a very developed system of values which was formed over a short period of time. The nepmen's system of values had many features in common with the system of values of pre-Revolutionary Russian merchants. Both of these social groups were similar in their attitude towards labour, wealth, state power, family, etc. Despite obvious similarities between nepmen's and merchants' systems of values, there were also essential distinctions which reveal the influence of the criminal world on nepmen. This influence of the criminal world became dominant at the end of the 1920s, and criminal values pushed out the other values from the nepmen's consciousness.

Nepmen strongly affected the other social groups. Towards the end of the 1920s, private entrepreneurs disappeared as a social group, but their system of values did not. Soviet people perceived some elements of this system. Thanks to nepmen the aspiration to the comfortable life became one of the main values of 'Soviet man'. Despite hard attempts, authorities could not eliminate this aspiration. Nepmen were also responsible for the emergence of a second important feature of the consciousness of Soviet people. The essence of this feature is captured in the famous adage 'To cheat the state, to gladden yourself'. The authorities unsuccessfully struggled with this feature throughout the Soviet period of history. To evaluate the influence of nepmen's system of values one can say that, generally speaking, it was positive. Nepmen brought a definite element of pragmatism into the too revolutionary for normal life consciousness of the Soviet people. This element of pragmatism made it closer to the reality.

NOTES

1. The whole body of historiography devoted to the Soviet private entrepreneurs-nepmen can be divided into two major groups: Soviet-Russian historiography and Western historiography. Although there is no great insurmountable gap between these two different historiographical traditions, Soviet and Western scholars who researched nepmen often came to similar conclusions, Western and Soviet historiography differed from each other. The approaches to the research, the topics of research, the methodology and even sources (Western scholars more often used periodicals and memoires, whereas Soviet historians mainly based their work on the records of bureaucratic organizations) were different in Western and Soviet historiography.

This gives us the grounds to examine Soviet and Western literature devoted to nepmen apart from each other.

The Soviet-Russian historiography of the NEP and nepmen went through three major stages of development. Each of these stages is characterised by changes in approach, topics and methods of research. A description of the peculiarities of each stage merits a further paper. Within this paper I only mark the chronological borders of every stage and indicate the most significant, from my point of view, books written on the theme of nepmen.

The first stage began immediately after the introduction of NEP. During the subsequent ten years many books devoted to the different aspects of the economic and social life of the NEP-society were written. See, Y. Larin, *Itogi, puti, vivodi NEPa* (Moscow, 1923); Y. Larin, *Chastniy kapital v SSSR* (Moscow, 1927); I. Mingulin, *Puti razvitiy chastnogo lawkapitila* (Moscow, 1927); I. Kondorushkin, *chastniy kapital pered sovetskim sudom* (Moscow, 1927); A. Fabrichniy, *Klassovay borba v gorode I gosudarstvennom apparate* (Moscow, 1930); N. Razanov, *Vitesnenie chastnogo posrednika iz tovarooborota* (Moscow, 1930). After the end of NEP and abolition of private entrepreneurship the study of these problems has practically ceased. The research work in this field was resumed only after Stalin's death and the introduction of Chrushev's 'thaw'. The 'thaw' initiated the second stage. See, I. Trifinof, *Likvidazia expluatatorskih klassov v SSSR* (Moscow, 1975); L. Morozov, *Reshaushiy etap borbi s nepmanskiy burzuaziey. Iz istorii likvidazii kapitalisticheskih elementov goroda* (Moscow, 1960); V. Arhipov, L. Morozov, *Borba protiv kapitalisticheskih elementov v promishlennosti I torgovle 20-e nechalo 30-h godov* (Moscow, 1978); V. Selunskay, *Izmenenie sozialniy structuri sovetskogo obshestva 1921-seredina 30-h godov* (Moscow, 1979).

The crucial changes in Russian historiography which occurred at the end of the 1980s also affected the historiography of NEP. It inititated the third stage which has been continues to the present. See, E. Horkova, *Istoria predprinimatelstva I meshanstva v Rosii* (Moscow, 1998); A. Kilin, *Chasnoe torgovoe predprinimatelstvo na Urale v godi NEPa* (Ekaterinburg, 1994); L. Lutov, *Chstnay promishlennost v godi NEPa* (Saratov, 1994); E. Demchik, *Chastniy kapital v gorodah Sibiri. Ot vozrozdeniy k likvidazii* (Baranaul, 1999); V. Ziromskay, *Posle revoluzionnih bur. Naselenie Rossii v pervoi polovine 20-h godov* (Moscow, 1996). In comparison with Soviet-Russian historiography, Western historiography paid much less attention to the problems of the NEP, which is quite natural. The history of nepmen was mainly explored by American historians in the research work dedicated to the social structure of Soviet society. See, E. Kimerling, 'Civil Rights and the social policy in the Soviet Russia, 1918–1936', *The Russian Review* (January, 1982); S. Fitzpatrik, *Klassi I problemi klassovoi prinadleznosti v Sovetskoi Rossii v 20-e godi in Voprosi istorii* (August, 1990); S. Fitzpatrick, 'Ascribing Class: the Construction of Social Identity on Soviet Russia', *Journal of Modern History* (April, 1993). From my point of view the best book written by a Western historian about nepmen is A. Ball, *Russian Last Capitalists* (California, 1987).

2. This paper is based on three groups of sources. The first group includes

archival materials. During the process of research the archives of organizations which to a greater or lesser degree came into contact with nepmen were
investigated. These organisations are the tax inspectors, courts, procurator's
office, banks, commodity exchanges, ministry of internal trade (NKVT),
ministry of industry (VSNH), local authorities, and, finally, the most valuable source – materials of OGPU. The second group of sources comprises
periodicals – central as well as regional. These periodicals are magazines
Vestnik finansov, Zizn Sibiri and newspapers *Izvestia, Ekonomicheskay Zizn,
Ekonomicheskay zizn Sibiri, Sovetskay zizn* and *Sovietskay Sisbir*. The third
group of sources includes memoires of people from different strata of society
– partly published and partly in manuscript.

The combination of these three groups of sources allows us to look on the
problem from different sides. It is necessary to say that our sources have one
significant defect. The majority of them focus on Siberia only. Probably the
situation in the other part of the USSR, particularly in the national districts,
was different from the situation in Siberia. However, we are taking a risk to
hypothesise that our conclusions concerning the nepmen's system of values
in Siberia are relevant for the entire social group of nepmen.

3. See, for example, N. Riauzov, *Vitesnenie Chastnogo posrednika iz
   tovarooborota* (Moscow, 1930); I. Trifonov, *Likvidazia ekspluatatorskih
   klassov v SSSR* (Moscow, 1975); E. Demchik, *Chasniy kapital v gorodah
   Sibiri v 1920-e godi: ot vozrozdeniy k likvidazii* (Barnaul, 1998)
4. State Archive of the Novosibirsk Region (SANR), collection 725, inventory
   1, file 39, p. 26.
5. Ibid, p. 26.
6. This point of view is accepted both by Soviet-Russian and Western
   historiography. See, for example, V. Selunskay, *Izmenenie sozialnioy struktyri
   sovetskogo obshestva: istoriay i sovremennost* (Moscow, 1979); E. Demchik,
   Chasniy kapital v gorodah Sibiri v 1920-e godi: ot vozrozdeniy k likvidazii
   (Barnaul, 1998); A Ball, *Russian Last Capitalists* (California, 1987).
7. Sovetskay Sibir 15 April 1923.
8. Sovetskay Sibir 28 October 1922.
9. Sovetskay Sibir, 9 January 1925.
10. Sovetskay Sibir, 18 February 1926.
11. Sovetskay Sibir, 9 January 1926.
12. SANR, c. 725, i. 1, f. 39, p. 21.
13. SANR, c. 659, i. 1, f. 286, p. 235; SANR, c. 918, i. 1, f. 185, p. 9–100.
14. SANR, c. 918, i. 1, f. 341, p. 43.
15. SANR, c. 918, i. 1, f. 200, p. 214 (back)
16. Sovetskay Sibir, 19 January 1927.
17. OGPU – *Osoboe Gosudarstvennoe Politicheskoe Upravlenie*. The heir of the
    notorious Cheka, political police in the Soviet Union in the 1920s.
18. SANR, c. 725, i. 1, f. 39.
19. SANR, c. 22, i. 1, f. 38, p. 46 (back).
20. Sovetskay Sibir, 28 April 1928.
21. T. Strizenova, *Iz istorii sovetskogo kostuma* (Moscow, 1972), p. 46.
22. Sovetskay Sibir, 7 May 1924.

23. W. Duranty, *Duranty Reports Russia* (New York, 1935), p. 108 quoted from A. Ball, *Russian Last Capitalists* (California, 1987), p. 41.
24. Sovetskay Sibir, 13 December 1924.
25. Sovtskay Sibir, 5 March 1927.
26. Sovetskay Sibir, 11 October 1922.
27. See, for example, Sovetskay Sibir or Sovetskaiy Zizn for any year since 1922 to 1929.
28. Sovetskay Sibir, 5 March 1927.
29. For the pre-Revolutionary merchants' system of values see, for example: V. Boiko, *Tomskoe kupechestvo* (Tomsk, 1996)
30. Counted by us. We explored the personal files of the private entrepreneurs of Novosibirsk in the SANR. The sample was 100 persons. According to the data of the head of the Siberian tax inspection (V. Kavrayski, 'Nalogooblozenie chastnogo capitala v Sibiri , Zizn Sibiri 5–6' (June-July 1924) 14) there were 907 private entrepreneurs in Novosibirsk in 1924. So the size of sample is 12 per cent of the general quantity. As the authors of the book *Lishenie izbiratelnih prav v Moskve v 1926–1930* (Moscow, 1997) who worked with analogous sources consider a sample to be representative if it is 10–15 per cent of the whole, we consider our sample to be representative.
31. E. Demchik, *Chastniy kapital v gorodah Sibiri. Ot vozrozdeniy k likvidazii* (Baranaul, 1999), p. 192.
32. See Sovetskay Sibir 4 April 1924; 13 December 1924; 16 January 1927; See also S. Kondorushkin, *Chastniy kapital pered sovetskim sudom* (Moscow, 1927).
33. Sovetskay Sibir, 20 February 1926.
34. SANR, c. 1021, i. 06, f. 9, p. 51.
35. Sovetskay Sibir, 11 May 1924.

The Four-Year Plan

Richard J. Overy

King's College, University of London

The popular historical judgement on the Second Four-Year Plan of September 1936 (so-called because it succeeded the rhetorical 'Four-Year Plan' for overcoming unemployment launched by Hitler in 1933) has generally followed the dismissive view expressed by Hjalmar Schacht in his memoirs: 'The Four-Year Plan brought relatively few positive results, apart from making a loud hoo-ha [*Brimborium*] about everything'. For Schacht the claims of those who ran the plan were vastly inflated: 'In the whole framework of economic policy', he announced to an audience of officers in 1937, 'the Four-Year Plan turns out to be only a small sector'.[1] For many post-war critics of the project it was neither properly planned, nor did it fulfil its Four-Year deadline. There is a common assumption that the plan was over-ambitious and unrealistic. By 1939, it is argued, Germany's dependence on foreign supplies, which the Plan was supposed to reverse, was almost unchanged from three years before: 20 per cent of foodstuffs and 33 per cent of raw materials. The plan organisation has been widely regarded as yet another example of the polycratic confusion of commissarial offices created, deliberately or otherwise, by a leader whose grasp of how to run a central government apparatus was at best primitive.

It is the contention of this article that the Four-Year Plan in fact represented a significant departure both for the German economy and for German politics, marking off the period of conservative collaboration and economic orthodoxy before 1936 from the period of economic imperialism, ethnic cleansing and military expansion that lasted to 1945. This is not the place to provide a detailed description of the origins and function of the Four-Year Plan, which have been thoroughly examined already.[2] The object is rather to explore the significance of the Plan through four separate but related arguments: first, that the Plan was conceived by Hitler not as a contribution to the alleged 'Darwinian' chaos of the state, but as the means to bring to an end just such a period of policy argument and jurisdictional confusion. Second, that the Plan in its establishment and early development has to be understood as much in political as in economic terms, as part of the political shift in the mid-1930s away from the conservative alliance towards more radical, Party-centred policies. Third, that the Plan was not simply a declaration of autarky, or self-sufficiency, but was part of a broader and more comprehensive strategy of *Wehrwirtschaft* for which autarky was merely a tactic. Fourth, that the Plan was not 'a small part of the economy', but stimulated a more general policy of macro-economic steering (like the Five-Year Plans in the USSR) which derived from the nature of *Wehrwirtschaft* itself. The net effect of the Plan was to produce a profound short-term re-structuring of the economy which went well beyond the trends already evident from the early years of the regime.

JURISDICTIONAL CHAOS AND THE FOUR-YEAR PLAN

The genesis of the Plan has to be understood against the background of Germany's economic relationship with the wider world economy since the slump and the impact that the early stages of remilitarisation had on that relationship. There was no alternative after 1933 to a policy of controlled trade in order to prevent economic recovery from placing pressure on the balance-of-payments and exposing how slight was the base of gold and foreign exchange on which the recovery was built. In September 1934 the *Neuplan* was introduced by the recently appointed Economics Minister, Hjalmar Schacht, which placed all trade and currency transactions under tight government regulation.

A year later, however, the pressure became more intense. A poor harvest made increased food imports necessary, yet the quickening pace of remilitarisation required additional foreign supplies of raw materials. Arguments over priority developed between the Food Estate, the armed forces and the Economics Ministry which were only temporarily suspended by the appointment of Hermann Göring (already President of the Reichstag and Minister of Aviation) first as an informal umpire between the competing claimants, then in April 1936 as Plenipotentiary for Raw Materials and Foreign Exchange. Over the summer months the arguments resumed more publicly as prominent spokesmen from business and politics entered the debate over economic strategy.[3] When Carl Goerdeler forwarded a memorandum to Hitler in August suggesting that the only solution to the economic crisis was to cut back on rearmament, a view consistent with Schacht's own judgement, Hitler responded by withdrawing to Berchtesgaden and penning the strategic memorandum that formed the basis of the Second-Four-Year Plan announced at the Party rally on 9 September 1936.[4]

Hitler's immediate purpose was to stifle the chorus of critical voices raised in the previous two or three months. He told the Party rally that he had long before come to recognise the 'gloomy pessimists' from 'bourgeois circles', but would not be deflected from his course.[5] For Hitler the only way to end the prolonged period of argument and jurisdictional confusion in economic policy was to impose a clear line of policy and to terminate the political struggles. A year before, at the 1935 Harvest Festival congress, he was already moving along a more dirigiste path: 'Without a plan we won't get by'.[6] The essence of the economic policy announced in September 1936 was what Hitler later called a *'planmäßige Lenkung'* (planned economic steering).[7]

The desire to end the period of policy chaos by imposing a clear set of policy objectives was only possible if there existed a source of political authority capable of imposing the economic strategy on the differing elements in the decision-making structure. The significant factor in Göring's appointment as Plenipotentiary for the Four-Year Plan was not only the nature of the individual chosen – a top Party personality, close to Hitler and one with a vested interest in promoting higher levels of remilitarisation – but the nature of the authority he was granted by Hitler. The decree announcing the formation of the Four-Year Plan organisation published on 18 October 1936 made evident Hitler's intention to create a single source of authority able to deliver the strategy outlined in the August memorandum. The decree was short and direct. The fulfilment of the Plan required 'a unitary direction of all the resources of the German people' and 'the tight co-ordination of all the specialist areas of responsibility in Party and State'.[8] The nature of Göring's authority was in a formal sense unlimited. When Göring discussed his new office in Cabinet on 21 October he warned his colleagues that their role was simply to recommend and advise, while he would use his *Vollmacht* to ensure that 'under all circumstances' the programmes of import substitution and rearmament were to be completed on the scale required.[9] When Heinrich Lammers, the Chancellery secretary, was asked after the war to explain the structure of authority following Göring's appointment he described it as follows

> The far-reaching authority of Göring, the Commissioner of the Four-Year Plan, under whose jurisdiction all Government and Party units were subordinated ... the Commissioner of the Four-Year Plan himself or through his executive in chief was always in a position to issue directives to the [Reich] Resorts. ... [10]

Of course, the mere assertion of authority did not guarantee that it would be exercised effortlessly and without friction. It took a further 18 months before Göring had become a virtual economic dictator, with the fusing of the Plan administration and the Reichswirtschaftsministerium and the appointment of the Party specialist Walther Funk as Economics Minister. What is significant about the decree appointing Göring and the *Vollmacht* it conferred upon him is not the outcome but the intention. The language used can be explained by the circumstances surrounding the policy and jurisdictional arguments of the summer of 1936. Hitler's motive, it appears, was not to contribute to the 'polycratic' confusion but instead to end the contest with the conservatives over economic strategy by bringing that confusion to an end. This conclusion raises serious doubts over the question of just how remote Hitler really was from the conduct of economic affairs. It also throws into doubt the view that Hitler encouraged administrative Darwinism as a deliberate political tactic.

THE 'PRIMACY OF POLITICS' UNDER THE FOUR-YEAR PLAN

Like Stalin's launch of the First Five-Year Plan in the Soviet Union in 1928, the Second Four-Year Plan had profound and unpredictable political consequences. Just as Stalin used the Soviet plan as an instrument for political realignment within the Communist Party and Soviet society to support both his personal dictatorship and a programme of economic radicalism, so the Four-Year Plan gave the opportunity to strengthen the role of the NSDAP in the apparatus of control and to undermine the consensus with the conservative elites established expediently in 1933.[11] The end of the period of policy compromise both strengthened Hitler's position as dictator and made possible the more radical programme of war preparation and territorial expansion that followed.

The consensus established in 1933 represented a compromise between the conservative circles in business and administration and the more moderate elements in the NSDAP, both of whom wanted economic revival and political stabilisation within a policy framework much of which had been anticipated well before Hitler became chancellor. There was general agreement that the German economy had to create some kind of post-liberal order based upon higher levels of state regulation, controlled trade and intervention in the capital sector. Some conservatives, though by no means all, welcomed the suppression of independent institutions of labour representation carried out in 1933. Both sides shared an economic nationalism forged in the 1920s; they wanted a restoration of German security through remilitarisation and an end to what they saw as a humiliating dependence on international finance. By spring 1936 recovery was statistically apparent; from that point on unemployment remained below the two million mark for the first time since 1928. The issue that challenged the initial consensus was the question of what recovery had been for. Schacht, one of the chief spokesmen for conservative opinion, wanted Germany to reengage with the world economy and encourage living-standard growth once a limited and affordable rearmament was completed some time in 1937/8.[12] Yet by 1936 it was apparent that the more radical economic nationalists in the Party wanted to increase German economic independence by promoting a higher degree of autarky and economic 'bloc building'. There emerged at the same time a renewed Party assault on 'economic egoism' and pressure to eradicate Jewish participation in business (which led to the first major wave of aryanisation in 1936/7), while the armed forces and Party militarists like Göring wanted to increase the tempo of rearmament.[13] Hitler shared much of this economic conception (it had been central to his strategic analysis in the so-called 'secret book' of 1929). He opted for the radical agenda of large-scale economic rearmament and autarky in the August memorandum, and Schacht became the German Bukharin.

The break-up of the consensus was already evident by the time of the Party rally in 1935 when Hitler pointed the way to higher levels of import-substitution. In a speech in Munich in December 1935 Schacht spoke out emphatically against the obsession with autarky and war-preparation. He rejected what he called '*die Autarkiefanatiker*'. Germany, he insisted, 'must affirm the idea of the world market and reject the idea of autarky', which leads only to impoverishment.[14] In the context of the time these were brave words. Press criticism of Schacht became widespread in 1936, while Hitler spoke more dismissively about him in private.[15] The armed forces were caught in the middle, since they did not want rearmament to slacken and had long argued for the necessity of producing a 'blockade-free' economy to avoid a repeat of the experience of the Great War. Their support for Schacht was weakened and the conservative front began to crumble. Businessmen were divided. While some, like the iron and steel owner Hermann Röchling, supported a more radical nationalist course, others, including the veteran industrialist Gustav Krupp, and the director of Vereinigte Stahlwerke, Ernst Poensgen, came out publicly in favour of Schacht's vision of expanded trade and limited armaments.[16]

The Party Rally of 1936, at which the Four-Year Plan was announced, was the point at which a more radical and instrumental view of the economy was openly declared. A few days later *Schwarze Korps*, the SS journal, announced that the Four-Year Plan could only be achieved 'to the extent that industry and economy are directed to the principles of the [National Socialist] movement'. The journal noted that the economy had not hitherto shown sufficient enthusiasm for the Party's *Weltanschauung*, and hinted at 'passive resistance' and 'sabotage'.[17] A few months later Hitler made his well-known Reichstag speech in which he warned the business community that 'National Socialism vigorously combats the opinion which holds that the economic structure exists for the benefit of capital ... '.[18]

The conflict continued into 1937. Although sections of the armed forces were able to work with the Four-Year Plan organisation, there was hostility to the loss of military control over the character and extent of rearmament and economic defence preparations. The War Minister, Werner von Blomberg, continued to make efforts to keep Schacht as a major player in economic policy, but his task was made more difficult by Schacht's open and persistent rejection of Göring's authority and of the autarkic strategy. The conflict was distilled in the struggle during 1937 to get the iron and steel industrialists to begin large-scale exploitation of domestic supplies of low-grade iron-ore. Almost certainly with Schacht's blessing, Ruhr business leaders rejected Göring's plans for domestic production. They found themselves outmanoeuvred politically; the ore-fields were nationalised, and their resistance treated by Göring as sabotage. Germany's senior economic elite found themselves subject to practices more reminiscent of the Soviet model – secret tape-recording of meetings, surveillance, threats of police terror.[19] Resistance evaporated by August 1937, and three months later Schacht formally resigned as Economics Minister, though Hitler insisted that he remains President of the Reichsbank perhaps from fear of the repercussions for foreign confidence in the currency, but more probably from fear that Schacht might become a rallying point for political opposition if he became fully independent of state responsibilities.[20]

Schacht took the opportunity afforded by his resignation to deliver a further stinging attack on the new economic direction in December 1937 in front of a military audience at the Wehrmachtakademie. He blamed growing rearmament and 'unproductive projects' [i.e. import substitution] for crowding out exports and reducing living-standard growth. The financial consequence was suppressed inflation and high government debt. The Four-Year Plan, Schacht continued, was technically inadequate and failed entirely to grasp the problems presented by an over-stretched economy and poor living standards. He concluded by reiterating his own solution: expansion of exports at all costs and a throttling back of all domestic projects funded by the state.[21] There is no doubt that if Schacht and his allies had won the contest over policy in 1936/7 German military and foreign policy too would have taken a very different course from 1938. He failed to win it not only because Hitler was prepared at the right moment to reject the conservative economic model (and the conservative alliance) in favour of building an economic empire backed by military force on a large scale, but also because Schacht lacked a sufficient political power base on which to found a more coherent opposition movement.

The result of the contest was the collapse of the political alliances of 1933. Between November 1937 and February 1938 Göring restructured the Economics Ministry by fusing his own Four-Year Plan Organisation with it, rather than continuing to depend entirely on the new organisational structure based on the Prussian State Ministry under Paul Körner.[22] Funk replaced Schacht in February, the same month that von Ribbentrop replaced von Neurath at the Foreign Office, and Hitler assumed supreme command of the armed forces following von Blomberg's resignation. Not all of these changes could be directly related to the Four-Year Plan, but the change in direction signalled by Hitler in the August memorandum, and repeated in the so-called Hossbach meeting on 5 November 1937, strained the conservative alliance to breaking point and brought a more radical political constellation to the fore, linked much more directly with Party circles.

THE FOUR-YEAR PLAN AND *WEHRWIRTSCHAFT*

The economic strategy behind the Four-Year Plan is usually characterised by the single word 'autarky'. This is a misleading description. Autarky was a tactic; the strategy was one of *Wehrwirtschaft* in which the highest possible self-sufficiency in foodstuffs and strategic raw materials (iron-ore, oil etc.) was regarded as one among a number of necessary objectives. Autarky itself was nothing new in 1936. Since the collapse of the world economy in the early 1930s the German economy had become progressively autarkic. In 1934 Germany depended for 25 per cent of her food and 35 per cent of raw materials on foreign supplies; in 1937 the figures were 17 per cent and 24 per cent respectively.[23] Imports as a proportion of the net national product were 16.5 per cent in 1932, but only 11.6 per cent in 1935, and 10.5 per cent in 1937. The output of domestically produced raw materials increased by 108 per cent between 1932 and 1937, but the supply of imported materials by only 14 per cent.[24] The production of natural oil, for example, from Germany's small and scattered oil fields was 102,900 tons in 1928, but had reached 318,000 tons by 1935 and 445,000 by 1936.[25]

The Four-Year Plan, it is well-known, intensified the development of import substitution through a large programme of investment in key areas – aluminium, synthetic textiles, synthetic rubber, oil from coal, domestic iron ore – but it was never intended to make Germany entirely independent of foreign supplies. 'We do not want to be isolated economically', wrote Göring in *Der Vierjahresplan*, the house journal. The object was to insulate Germany from the effects of the world economy as a precondition for its military security. Trade was to be closely controlled to allow the economy to achieve its 'national tasks'.[26] One of those tasks was widely perceived to be the construction of a new economic order to replace the defunct liberal trading system. For economic nationalists this meant the widely-discussed idea of a system of closed economic blocs (*Großraumwirtschaft*) in which a form of 'regional' autarky might be established. No contradiction was seen between the pursuit of autarky domestically and the development of the large economic area, predominantly self-sufficient and rationally organised to meet German interests.[27] Indeed autarky and economic imperialism were regarded as complementary.

Autarky was in this sense a function of the wider search for an economic strategy that could provide security, not only from the vicissitudes of the world market, but from the dangers Germany faced in the event of an international conflict in which blockade was once again a weapon. This strategy, usually described by the term *Wehrwirtschaft*, was based, like most war economies, on a crude productionist conception of the economy. 'The salvation of our people', Hitler told the Reichstag in January 1937, 'is not a problem of finances, but exclusively a problem of the exploitation and mobilisation of our available labour force and the exploitation of the available earth and the earth's riches'.[28] Those who advocated *Wehrwirtschaft* were very aware that between 1914 and 1918 Germany had not made the most of the resources available, a failure largely attributed to the lack of effective pre-war preparation. Since the 1920s the German armed forces had argued the case for the systematic preparation of the physical economy for conversion to an effective war economy in the event of a major conflict. Hitler shared this conception entirely; the August memorandum was in essence a declaration that economic policy was to be governed by the principles of *Wehrwirtschaft*.

In its simplest terms the concept amounted to little more than the idea that a major power engaged in war should have so ordered its economic situation that it would be capable of supplying weapons and food in sufficient quantities to keep the armed forces fighting and the population fed.[29] This was, in reality, a far from simple strategy. It involved control over trade to ensure priority for strategic imports, the build-up of domestic supplies of vital materials, the control of prices and wages to prevent domestic consumer pressure from generating inflation, the re-training of labour in skills appropriate to defence purposes, and the steering of the industrial economy to create the capacity for the output of high quality machine-engineering and chemical products capable of rapid conversion to war production. The interlocking character of the elements of a modern industrial system explains why it was regarded as necessary to regulate all the major economic variables in order to achieve the security objective.

This was the strategy adopted under the Second Four-Year Plan. Some of it was already in place, for example the controls over foreign trade and payments, because of the circumstances dictated by the slump. What the Four-Year Plan signified was the recognition that left to itself an economy emerging slowly from a disastrous slump with strong pressure to revive the consumer sectors would not of its own accord create the framework of economic rearmament necessary to ensure German security. As a later report on the activity of the Plan admitted

> The preparatory work in the summer [of 1936] had already shown that not only the technical and production questions had to be solved to fulfil the Führer's commission, but that to achieve the goal it would require the complete mobilisation of all economic resources and a broad reconstruction of the existing economic system.[30]

That goal was, according to Erich Neumann, State Secretary in the re-organised Economics Ministry, 'the radical adaptation of the former liberal national economy from the principle of international division of labour to the principle of military economic security'.[31]

Hitler's interests, of course, went beyond the establishment of defensive security and economic insulation to embrace the active preparation for war and territorial expansion for which the Plan organisation had ultimate responsibility. Autarky had some role to play in this, although Hitler later commented that the autarkic programme had been pushed too far once it was manifest how easily additional resources could simply be seized by force.[32] The essence of active economic preparation for war remained *Wehrwirtschaft*. This is evident from the discussions and subsequent instructions issued by Göring as Four-Year Plan Plenipotentiary that followed the announcement from Hitler's headquarters (OKW) in June 1938 of 'gigantic new tasks' in Reich defence. These discussions not only concerned autarkic issues of trade, foreign exchange and domestic import-substitution, but embraced cuts in consumption growth, tighter controls over the labour market, restrictions on social expenditures ('however desirable or necessary they might be'), more closely controlled raw material allocation and the production and distribution of foodstuffs.[33] This range of activities inevitably involved the Four-Year Plan in more comprehensive economic steering, and explains the views of its key officials that the Plan had ultimately to impose 'full control over the economy' if its specific purposes were to be fulfilled.[34]

THE FOUR-YEAR PLAN AND THE 'MANAGED ECONOMY'

There developed a close connection between the activity of the Four-Year Plan organisation and the evolution of dirigiste economic policies. Contemporary economists defined the system as a 'managed economy' (*gelenkte Wirtschaft*). This outcome can partly be explained by the fact that the strategy of economic rearmament had implications for all the major economic variables. The different elements in the operation of a *Wehrwirtschaft* were in no sense discrete, for they depended on other parts of the system operating in synthesis. It can also be explained by the slow emergence of a system of macro-economic steering under the impact of the slump, which provided many of the policy instruments later exploited by the Plan (and also anticipated the more interventionist European economies developed after 1945). There is now a growing recognition that German economists and economic officials in the early 1930s already understood much of what came later to be called 'Keynesianism'. In reaction to the apparent collapse of economic liberalism, economists in Germany explored the theoretical basis for *Wirtschaftslenkung* as an alternative. This economic discourse was mobilised in the mid-1930s to help officials and Party economists to try to understand the nature and consequences of the new forms of economic management. Macro-economic steering required a proper understanding of the processes at work in an economic system even in a dictatorship.[35]

Figure 1: Main Organisational Structure of the Four-Year Plan

I   Organisation according to decree of 23 October 1936
      General Council
      Central Secretariat
      Main Divisions (Geschäftsgruppen)
            1   Production of German raw and work materials
            2   Raw Material Distribution
            3   Labour
            4   Agricultural production
            5   Price formation
            6   Foreign Exchange

II Organisation according to decree 26 November 1937, in operation
      from 4 February 1938
      General Council
      Central Secretariat
      Four-Year Plan Divisions
            1   Price formation
            2   Labour
            3   Agricultural Production
      Four-Year Plan Divisions/RWM Departments
            1   German raw and work materials
            2   Foreign exchange, exports
            3   Mining, iron, energy supply
            4   Currency and credit
            5   Trade and commerce

Source: Kölble, *Arbeitskraft*, p. 193; Petzina, *Autarkie*, pp.60,65

The central elements of the 'managed economy' were controls over price formation and wages, the regulation of physical resources (raw materials, semi-finished products) and trade. These areas of policy-formation were brought under the umbrella of the Four-Year Plan during 1936 and 1937 [see Figure 1], and then shared with the re-organised Economics Ministry in 1938. Most of the personnel who occupied key posts in the Plan organisation were housed in the Leipzigerstraße in Berlin, either in, or close to, the Prussian State Ministry where Göring had his civilian head-quarters. Some were recruited from the career civil service, some from business and accountancy, some from Party circles. The organisation quickly built up a substantial bureaucracy to cope with its regulatory and planning functions. Up to the outbreak of war the Plan was overseen by a General Council which met regularly to discuss and co-ordinate policy across the whole range of economic issues. An inner circle of the Council also met regularly. The nominal head of the new structure was Paul Körner, but those who worked in the organisation regarded his deputies Erich Neumann and Friedrich Gramsch as the real driving force who, so it was claimed, 'long into the war steered the entire economy'.[36] Göring relied heavily on the help of the experts but was by no means a silent partner. Up to the outbreak of war the minutes reveal a leader with a grasp of the issues and the ambition to impose policy. The macro-economic strategy did not emerge in the form of a single predictive plan along Soviet lines, though there was central planning of the production, import and distribution of materials, which had an impact throughout the economy. The control over physical resources and their distribution allowed the regime to regulate the balance between producer and consumer goods and to compel the civilian consumer economy to grow more slowly than the growth of aggregate earnings might have allowed. Favourable treatment for heavy industry and engineering encouraged the redistribution of investment in favour of industries important for war, while the throttling back of consumption encouraged increased savings which the regime mobilised via the banking system for its own expenditure on military preparations. This circular system ensured that the government got access to loan funds to pay for rearmament from consumers who could not buy increased consumer goods because of the allocation of priority in the first place to war-related projects.[37]

In order to work, the system required a policy of price formation, which could be manipulated to avoid open inflation. The Commissar for Price Formation was appointed under the Four-Year Plan on 29 October 1936 with very broad instructions to regulate prices for all goods and services, in particular 'all necessities of daily life'.[38] The choice as commissar fell on Josef Wagner, Gauleiter of Silesia, who had a reputation as a tough enforcer. He was armed with comprehensive powers through the 'price-stop' decree of 26 November. All price increases had to be reported to the network of price control offices established across the Reich. They could be approved only after accounting staff had satisfied themselves that the cost-structure of the business justified the increase. Since wages were an important component in prices, Wagner insisted that wage increases be notified to him as well. Gradually the price commissar's office was able to affect price formation by recommending to businesses ways of rationalising their practices to reduce costs and stabilise prices.[39] Robert Ley, head of the Deutsche Arbeitsfront, described Wagner's office as 'a sort of economic Reich Chancellery'. Although other ministries and businesses co-operated reluctantly with Wagner's organisation (firms disliked the requirement to open up their cost accounting methods to public scrutiny), it became one of the critical elements in the new structure of economic steering.[40] Some of its provisions remained in force after 1949.

The pricing policies were closely linked with the micro-economy where limitations on consumer spending were essential to allow the diversion of resources to war-related projects. It has often been argued that Hitler intended to provide both 'guns and butter' before 1939 because of fears of consumer protest. In reality with the introduction of the Plan in 1936 no effort was made to mask from the public the fact that economic restructuring could only be achieved at the expense of living-standard growth. 'For us the Four-Year Plan is not concerned now with the production of finished goods and consumer products, which only help to produce a more pleasant standard of life', ran one commentary on the proclamation of the Plan.[41] In 1941 Erich Neumann told an audience at the Verwaltungs-akadamie that the Plan had never been intended at the outset as a means to benefit consumers: 'Before we can begin to favour consumption, the fundamentals of national economy will have to be reestablished and permanently secured ... 'Guns instead of butter' is the watchword that hits the nail on the head'.[42]

The limitation of living standard growth was nonetheless a difficult policy to maintain. It was undertaken through an extensive propaganda campaign which aimed to encourage saving, to reduce waste and excess and to promote a conscious understanding that 'national tasks' had to take priority over consumer interests. In its most direct form the work of the Plan was brought into every household through the decrees on recycling and waste issued during the first year of the Plan. Starting with the Decree on Kitchen Waste [*Küchenabfälle-Erlaß*] published on 20 November 1936, there followed decrees on household refuse, paper recycling, raw material recycling, and a general decree on 12 November 1937 on the disposal of all other materials.[43] Regular visits from the Hitler Youth or the SA collecting contributions for the cause of autarky were a sharp reminder at the humblest economic level of the priorities of the new economic regime, and a convenient, if trivial, way of inducing social commitment to the goals of the Plan. Failure to support recycling could be legally interpreted as sabotage.[44] The effectiveness of this campaign was revealed in the aftermath of the *Kristallnacht* pogrom when complaints were heard that the destruction ran entirely counter to the spirit and letter of the Four-Year Plan.[45]

THE FOUR-YEAR PLAN IN PERSPECTIVE

The origins and development of the Second Four-Year Plan had important implications for the nature of economic policy-making. The Plan brought the extensive programmes for *Wehrwirtschaft*, hitherto under military supervision, under a central civilian organisation that gradually assumed responsibility for a more general macro-economic steering in order to achieve the war-related goals which were its *raison d'être*. At the same time the Plan was exploited as a means to overcome the resistance and hostility of conservative opponents of rearmament, import-substitution and aryanisation. The changes associated with the Plan were substantial, both in terms of the ambitious short-term restructuring of a large and technically advanced industrial economy and in terms of the political conflicts which surrounded its introduction and implementation. Under these circumstances it is unsurprising that the Four-Year Plan, like its Five Year equivalent in the Soviet Union, did not achieve everything it set out to. It would be a mistake, however, to assume as a result that the Plan was a mere facade or an expensive failure. The evidence from the period 1936 to 1939, both at the level of the macro- and micro-economy, demonstrates that the Plan did play a central part in distorting Germany's economic structure in favour of *Wehrwirtschaft* and in controlling the social and economic consequences of doing so.

The balance between the producer and consumer sectors, which had already tilted in favour of heavy industry in the first years of recovery, moved even more sharply away from the consumer sectors [see Table 1]. By 1938 the proportion of industrial incomes earned in the consumer sector was 25 per cent and the proportion of investment in consumer goods only 17 per cent of the whole; in 1933 the figures had been 37 and 41 per cent respectively. A Reichsbank memorandum observed unfavourably that the 1938 figures showed the same proportion as the Soviet economy.[46] In fact the relationship between consumer and producer goods was even less favourable than the raw data suggest. First, the absolute quantity of investment in consumer goods was still, in nominal terms, 20 per cent below the level for 1929, whereas investment in producer goods was 25 per cent higher. Second, some firms classified under the heading consumer industries had by 1939 devoted some or all of their production to goods for the armed forces, either by converting to war products, or through the supply of consumer goods for military use. The proportion of goods available for the civilian consumer market was lower than the aggregate of goods produced by 'consumer industries', often by a wide margin.[47]

Table 1: Wage Costs and Investment in German Industry 1929–38 (billion RM)

	Total Wage Costs		Investment	
Year	Producer Goods	Consumer Goods	Producer Goods	Consumer Goods
1929	9.45	3.82	1.993	0.620
1930	7.16	3.60	1.093	0.476
1931	4.81	3.10	0.590	0.289
1932	3.18	2.21	0.264	0.175
1933	3.74	2.18	0.329	0.228
1934	5.50	2.53	0.734	0.326
1935	6.69	2.56	1.271	0.365
1936	7.79	2.78	1.705	0.452
1937	9.00	3.12	2.169	0.489
1938	10.06	3.37	2.500*	0.500*

* provisional figure

Source: BAB (Archive of the Federal Republic of Germany, Berlin) R 2501/6585, Deutsche Reichsbank, Steigende Löhne, knappe Verbrauchsgüter, 24 August 1939, Anlage 1.

The figures for investment as a whole reveal other significant evidence of restructuring. Industrial investment as a proportion of all investment was 18 per cent in 1927/9, but 24 per cent in 1937/9. Four-Year Plan investments represented 53 per cent of all industrial investment in 1937 and 1938 and 48 per cent in 1939. Together with other forms of war-related investment (for example in the aircraft industry) the proportion of all industrial investment in war-related projects has been estimated at more than 60 per cent between 1936 and 1939.[48] Investment was undertaken by mobilising a mixture of public and private funds, helped by a sharp improvement in the savings ratio (6.7 per cent 1929, 14.3 per cent 1936). The sums authorised in 1936 and 1937 for Four-Year Plan projects are presented in Table 2. Most of the investment was undertaken in iron and steel, chemicals, non-precious metals, and shipping. There were also sub-

Table 2: Four-Year Plan Financial Planning, 1937–40 (billion RM)

	1937	1938	1939	1940	Total
Plan, Jan 1937	3.018	3.461	1.490	0.642	8.611
Plan, Feb 1937	1.832	2.022	1.013	0.983	5.850
Plan, May 1937	2.864	2.864	1.844	0.833	8.405
Plan, Dec 1937	1.461	2.393	2.724	2.232	8.810
Actual expend.	1500	1950	2.100	2.490	8.040
% of all industrial					
investment	53.5	52.7	47.7	58.0	52.9

Source: BAK (Archive of the Federal Republic of Germany, Koblenz) R 25/84–5, Reichsamt fur Wirtschaftsausbau, Finanzbedarf der Projekte des Vierjahresplanes, 12 July 1938; BAB R 3101/17789, RWM Finanzplan, n.d [January 1937]; RWM Aktenvermerk, 15 February 1937; Petzina, *Autarkiepolitik*, p.183 for statistics on actual expenditure.

stantial sums allocated for canal building and energy supply[49] [see Table 3].

The net effect of the strategy to shift national resources away from consumption and trade in order to free capacity for 'national' projects, particularly (but not exclusively) war preparation, was presented by an official of the former Reich Statistical Office in a paper drawn up in 1947. It was calculated that additional tax revenues, falling unemployment payments and public loans made available for the government a total of 86.3 billion *RM* between 1932 and August 1939. Of this figure some 57.8 billion *RM* (67 per cent) was spent on remilitarisation in all its forms; much of the rest was spent on prestige projects such as the *Reichsautobahnen* and the city rebuilding.[50] By 1939 projects worth an estimated 30 billion *marks* remained uncompleted.[51] At this point 50 *pfennig* of every *mark* spent by the government went towards the direct military budget; the additional amount spent on indirect forms of economic rearmament has yet to be calculated.[52] All of these sums reduced very substantially the margin available to increase the well-being of the population at large. Against a real net national product growth of 48 per cent between 1929 and 1938, real per capita consumption rose by only four per cent. The Four-Year Plan absorbed a high proportion of the remainder of that growth: guns, and a great deal more, before butter.

This is not to deny that the Plan created additional problems for the German economy because of the tension between the macro-economic priorities and the micro-economic reality of slow labour retraining schemes, shortages of skilled labour, increased job mobility and a slow decline in productivity growth as firms found themselves under less pressure to cut

Table 3: Allocation of Four-Year Plan Investment by Sector, Plan I, 10 Jan
1937 (Mill. RM)

Sector	1937	1938	1939	1940	1941
Group I					
Textiles	86	29	17	–	–
Non-precious metals	105	118	103	31	–
Iron and Steel	90	85	38	18	13
Fat-free wash materials	19	38	–	–	–
Tanned goods	10	10	3	–	–
Soot	8	9	–	–	–
Sausage skins	2	–	–	–	–
Rubber	215	220	80	–	–
Mineral oil	463	642	220	115	–
Chemicals (from wood)	17	1	–	–	–
Wood	5	4	2	–	–
Foodstuffs	32	32	29	22	–
Canal-building	186	265	265	265	–
Shipbuilding	196	356	200	111	–
Group II (additional programme)					
Synthetic textiles	170	38	–	–	–
Wood	65	95	57	11	–
Group III					
Coal	16	24	3	–	–
Energy supply	313	324	243	69	–
Chemicals	869	1122	230	–	–
Technical products	151	49	–	–	–
Total investment	3018	3461	1490	642	13

Source: BAB R 3101/17789, RWM, Auszug aus dem Rohstoffplan, January 1937

costs in an environment of government contracts and protection from the
world market. All of these problems stemmed from the decision to turn
Germany into a military-economic superpower in a short period of time
using a form of *Wirtschaftslenkung* which was in an almost permanently
experimental state. In February 1940 Dr. Tomberg, a member of the OKW
Wehrwirtschafts- und Rüstungsstab, wrote an assessment of Germany's
current war economic situation in the light of the work of the Four-Year
Plan in which he blamed the existing problems in the war economy on the

persistent 'dualism of military and civilian offices', which between them had 'already in peacetime as a result of constantly excessive claims used up the important reserves essential for war'.[53] In this sense the Four-Year Plan and the strategy of rapid and extensive economic rearmament had been too successful for its own good.

The Four-Year Plan symbolised the transition in Germany from a conservative strategy for economic revival regulated by 'bourgeois experts' to a massively militarised and regulated economy closely linked to Party circles and animated increasingly by a more radical ideological agenda. This agenda was expressed through the drive for living space, programmes of aryanisation and, ultimately, through war and conquest. Its significance derived not only from its extensive, and often underestimated, economic programmes, but from the wider political role it performed in altering the balance of power between elites and in mobilising popular sources of economic nationalism to sustain and legitimate the loss of individual wellbeing in the name of 'national economic tasks', of which the Plan was the most obtrusive.

NOTES

1. Bundesarchiv-Berlin (BAB), R 2501/7031, Vortrag des Dr. Schacht vor der Wehrmachtakademie, 10 December 1937, p. 25; H. Schacht, 76 Jahre meines Lebens (Bad Wörishofen, 1954), p. 465. On the First Four-Year Plan see A.I. Berndt, Gibt mir Vier Jahre Zeit (Munich, 1937), pp. 211–2.
2. See in particular D. Petzina, Autarkiepolitik im Dritten Reich (Stuttgart, 1968); M. Riedel, Eisen und Kohle für das Dritte Reich: Paul Pleigers Stellung in der nationalsozialistischen Wirtschaft (Göttingen, 1973); E. Teichert, Autarkie und Großraumwirtschaft in Deutschland 1930–1939 (Munich, 1984).
3. R.J. Overy, Goering: the 'Iron Man' (London, 1984), pp. 38–43.
4. Völkischer Beobachter, 10 September 1936, p. 56 for full text of the speech.
5. W. Treue, "Die Denkschrift Hitlers über die Aufgaben eines Vierjahresplans", Vierteljahreshefte für Zeitgeschichte, 3 (1954), p. 191.
6. Bundesarchiv-Koblenz (BAK) R7/ 2149, Ohlendorf papers, "Grundsätze der Volkswirtschaftspolitik" n.d. [assumed October 1935], p. 9. (Documents referred to under the signature BA/K have now been transferred to the Bundesarchiv in Berlin. I have used the old references here for more convenient identification)
7. Berndt, Gibt mir Vier Jahre Zeit, p. 235.
8. Reichsgesetztblatt, 1936, Part I, p. 887.
9. BAK R26 IV/4, Sitzung des kleinen Ministerrats, 21 October 1936, p. 2. The minutes noted: 'Was die Durchführung anlangt, so ist die Vollmacht des Ministerpräsidenten [Göring] nicht beschränkt'.
10. Imperial War Museum, London, FO 645, Box 159, Heinrich Lammers, 'Notes on Legislation and Measures for the Defence of the Reich', 17 October 1945, p. 7.

11. There is interesting discussion of the political conflicts arising out of the economic plans in the USSR in J. Haslam, 'Political Opposition to Stalin and the Origins of the Terror in Russia, 1932–1936', *The Historical Journal*, 29 (1986) pp. 395–418; on the economic consequences see M.R. Dohan, 'The Economic Origins of Soviet Autarky 1927/8–1934', *Slavic Review*, 35 (1976), pp. 603–35.

12. See for example BAK R2501/7034, Schacht press conference, 30 September 1936. Schacht used the conference with foreign journalists to press his case for expanded trade and exports (and the return of German colonies) as a key to higher livings standards, a direct challenge to the purposes behind the recent announcement of the Four-Year Plan.

13. On the issue of aryanisation see the pioneering study by F. Bajohr, *"Arisierung" in Hamburg: die Verdrängung der jüdischen Unternehmer 1933–1945* (Hamburg, 1997), who argues that pressure for formal procedures for aryanisation increased conspicuously in 1936/7. When Göring announced the Four-Year Plan at the Berlin Sportpalast on October 18 1936 he described the German economy of the Weimar years 'cleaned out and plundered by the Jews' (E. Gritzbach (ed.), *Hermann Göring: Reden und Aufsätze* (Munich, 1938), p. 258; the Plan was later described as a means to free Germany 'from international Jewry, from businessmen alien to the *Volk*, from monopolists ... ' (W. Jungermann, H. Krafft, *Rohstoffreichtum aus deutscher Erde* (Berlin, 1939), p. 10).

14. R 2501/3795, Vortrag Dr. Schachts vor dem Bund der Freunde der Technischen Hochschule, Munich 7 December 1935, p. 10, 14.

15. F. Hossbach, *Zwischen Wehrmacht und Hitler 1934–1938* (Göttingen, 1965), pp. 31–2.

16. On Röchling see D. Eichholtz, W. Schumann (eds.), *Anatomie des Krieges* (Berlin, 1969), pp. 142–3, doc. 47, Denkschrift vom 17 August 1936, "Gedanken über die Vorbereitung zum Kriege und seine Durchführung"; on Krupp see IWM, Krupp collection, Privatakten: Reden, Rede für Jubilärfeier, Grusonwerk, Magdeburg, 30 May 1935; on Poensgen, BAK R 26 I/30, Keppler Tageszettel 5 October 1936.

17. BAB R 2501/3795, "Nun aber handeln!", *Schwarze Korps*, 8 October 1936, p. 1.

18. N. Baynes, *Hitler's Speeches* (2 vols, Oxford, 1942) ii, p. 935, speech to the Reichstag, 30 January 1937.

19. See R.J. Overy, 'Heavy Industry and the State in Nazi Germany: the Reichswerke Crisis', *European History Quarterly*, 15 (1985), pp. 317–23; H. Gisevius, *To the Bitter End* (London, 1948) pp. 201–2 relates the efforts he made on Schacht's behalf to find the hidden Gestapo microphones in Schacht's apartment as early as 1935.

20. There is an interesting testimony on the events surrounding Schacht's continued appointment at the Reichsbank in IWM FO 645, Box 159, Lammers interrogation, 17 October 1945. Lammers suggested that Hitler kept Schacht in office because he did not want Schacht to have the right to say when he would or would not undertake his duties. Lammers recalled Hitler's remark: 'I must have the right of action in my own hands'.

21. BAB R 2501/7031, Vortrag Dr. Schachts vor der Wehrmachtakademie, pp. 1–6, 27, 30.
22. Kölble, *Arbeitskraft schafft Wirtschaftsfreiheit* (Leipzig, 1938) pp. 193–4 on the organisational changes from 1936 to 1938; also Petzina, *Autarkiepolitik*, pp. 60, 65–7.
23. Kölble, *Arbeitskraft*, p. 17.
24. L. Zumpe, *Wirtschaft und Staat in Deutschland 1933 bis 1945* (Berlin, 1979), p. 221; H.E. Volkmann, 'Die NS-Wirtschaft in Vorbereitung des Krieges' in W. Deist et al., *Das Deutsche Reich und der Zweite Weltkrieg: Band I* (Stuttgart, 1979), p. 262.
25. Jungermann, Krafft, *Rohstoffreichtum*, p. 69.
26. E. von Mickwitz, *Außenhandel unter Zwang* (Hamburg, 1938), p. 5.
27. See for example the arguments in H. Kremmler, *Autarkie in der organischen Wirtschaft* (Dresden, 1940) pp. 74–5; V. Muthesius, *Europas Autarkie* (Berlin, n.d. [1941?]) who argued that 'German autarky in its properly understood sense can only achieve its full realisation above all in the framework of a comprehensive European autarky.'
28. Berndt, *Gibt mir vier Jahre Zeit*, p. 234.
29. On contemporary views of the concept see for example G. Thomas [Chief of the Wehrwirtschafts- und Rüstungsamt], "Die Verantwortung in der Wehrwirtschaft", *Der deutsche Volkswirt*, 10 (1936), pp. 1320–2; Major Hesse, "Über die Grenzen der Wehrwirtschaft" *DDV*, 10 (1936), pp. 1591–2.
30. BAK R 26 I/18, Ergebnisse der Vierjahresplan-Arbeit, spring 1942, p. 2.
31. IWM Nuremberg Trials, Case XI, Pros. Doc. Book 112, 'The Four-Year Plan', lecture delivered before the Verwaltungsakademie, 29 April 1941, p. 2.
32. IWM EDS papers, Chef Wi-Rü Amt [Thomas], Aktennotiz, 20 June 1941: "Der Verlauf des Krieges zeigt, dass wir in unseren autarkischen Bestrebungen zu weit gegangen sind ... Man muss einen anderen Weg gehen und muss das, was man benötigt und nicht hat erobern ... ".
33. National Archives, Washington DC, microcopy T177 Roll 71, frames 791892–97, Göring to all Reich ministers 'betr. Reichsverteidigung'; frames 791899–901, Göring to Darré, 22 June 1938; frames 791903–08, Göring to Funk, 22 June 1938.
34. IWM, Case XI, Pros. Doc. Book 112, Report from Loeb to Göring, 30 Oct 1937, 'Results of work done during the first year of the Four-Year Plan', p. 79.
35. See for example H. Janssen, *Nationalökonomie und Nationalsozialismus: die deutsche Volkswirtschaftslehre in den dreißiger Jahren* (Marburg, 1998), esp. pp. 463–505; H. Woll, *Die Wirtschaftslehre des deutschen Faschismus* (Munich, 1988); W. Krause, G. Rudolph, *Grundlinien des ökonomischen Denkens in Deutschland 1848 bis 1945* (Berlin, 1980), pp. 433– 69.
36. BAK R 26 II Anh./2, W. Rentrop, Materialen zur Geschichte des Reichskommissars für die Preisbildung, pp. 8–13.
37. For the effects on living standards see BAB R 2501/6585, Deutsche

Reichsbank, 'Steigende Löhne, knappe Verbrauchsgüter', 24 Aug 1939, pp. 6–7.
38. *Reichsgesetzblatt*, 1936 Part I, p. 927.
39. BAK R 26 II Anh./1, H. Dichgans, 'Zur Geschichte des Reichskommissars für die Preisbildung' n.d., pp. 4–6, 9–11; R 26 II Anh./2, pp. 12–18.
40. BAK R 26 II Anh./1, p. 4.
41. Jungermann, Krafft, *Rohstoffreichtum*, p. 10.
42. IWM, Case XI Pros. Doc. Book 112, Neumann lecture, p. 294.
43. BAB R 3102/3602, Statistisches Reichsamt, A. Jessen, 'Die gesteuerte Wehrwirtschaft 1933–1939', 25 February 1947, p. 61.
44. J. Stephenson, 'Propaganda, Autarky and the German Housewife' in D. Welch (ed.), *Nazi Propaganda: the Power and the Limitations* (London, 1983), pp. 117–42.
45. P. Freimark, W. Kopitzsch, *Der 9/10 November 1938 in Deutschland* (Hamburg, 1988), p. 80.
46. BAB R 2501/6585, Deutsche Reichsbank, „Steigende Löhne, knappe Verbrauchsgüter', 24 August 1939, p. 7.
47. Volkmann, 'Die NS-Wirtschaft', pp. 313–4 provides a detailed breakdown of the proportion of industrial sales by sector represented by military orders in July 1937. Most major consumer sectors devoted from 10 to 20 per cent of their output for military orders. For the Statistisches Reichsamt there was no easy way to distinguish between consumer production for the civilian and military markets and all consumer industry production remained classified as 'consumer goods' even during the war when the proportion going to the military was in some sectors well in excess of 50 per cent.
48. Petzina, *Autarkiepolitik*, pp. 183–5.
49. BAB R 3101/17789, RWM, 'Finanzierungsplan' n.d. [January 1937], Appendix 1.
50. BAB R 3102/3602, Jessen, 'Gesteuerte Wehrwirtschaft', pp. 131–5. The figures given for military spending are as follows:

Direct Wehrmacht expenditure	48.7 billion RM
Rearmament expenditure of civil authorities	4.5
Arbeitsdienst	2.0
Rearmanent expenditure of NSDAP	0.6
Miscellaneous sums	2.0

These sums exceed the figures conventionally given for military spending.
51. Zumpe, *Wirtschaft und Staat*, p. 258. Zumpe calculates total public investment and military spending at 69.67 billion RM from 1933 to 1938, which represented 68 per cent of the total.
52. NA Microcopy T178, Roll 15, frame 3671912, Reichsfinanzministerium, 'Statistische Über-sichten zu den Reichshaushaltsrechnungen 1938 bis 1943', November 1944.
53. NA Microcopy T77, Roll 80, frames 803161–2, Dr. Tomberg, 'Deutschlands Wehrwirtschaftspotential bei Kriegsausbruch', 26 February 1940, pp. 1–2.

State Owned Enterprises: Hitler's Willing Servants? The Decision-making Structures of VIAG (Vereinigte Industrieunternehmungen AG) and RKA (Deutsche Rentenbank-Kreditanstalt)[1]

Andrea H. Schneider

Association for Business History, Frankfurt am Main

INTRODUCTION

Discussions about state-owned companies during the Nazi period assume, understandably, that these firms were easily penetrated by the Nazis, that they followed the Nazi policies in every respect and that at least they voluntarily became simple instruments of the regime. But closer examination reveals a variety of behavioural patterns in state-owned enterprises. This paper illustrates the complexity of relationships between the State and state-owned enterprises with two examples: Vereinigte Industrieunternehmungen AG (VIAG),[2] a state-owned holding company, which was among Germany's 25 largest companies in 1938,[3] and Deutsche Rentenbank-Kreditanstalt (RKA), a public institution created to promote agriculture.[4]

Based on their structures, however, the industrial holding company (VIAG) and the agrarian bank (RKA) do not seem comparable. Nevertheless, both firms played an important role in their sectors, whose importance grew for the National-Socialist regime as the German economy became more devoted to military needs during the mid-thirties (*Rüstungswirtschaft*). VIAG's electricity and aluminium divisions were essential to Hitler's autarky policy. The agriculture sector's long-term financial problems increased the importance of agrarian credits (*Agrarkredit*), especially as autarky and armament policies came to dominate the economy.[5] The debts of the agriculture sector, which in 1927 amounted to 5.1 billion RM, by 1933, had climbed to 14.0 billion RM.[6] Hitler's ambition to create an autarkical economic system needed vibrant energy, nitrogen and electricity production as well as a well-functioning system for financing agriculture to overcome Germany's backwardness in this sector.[7] The special combination of being public or state owned with playing major roles in each of the branches led to a preferential treatment in co-operation with Göring's

'Four-Year Plan'-bureaucracy (*Behörde des Vierjahrsplanes*). This paper will present the economic circumstances, the political background and the reactive scope of these enterprises just prior to and after the *Machtergreifung*. It is an attempt to uncover similarities and structures, networks and relationships behind the co-operation between the State and its enterprises.

THE FOUNDING OF VIAG AND RKA DURING THE 1920s

Both of these public institutions were created in the mid-1920s. This was not purely by coincidence but rather the consequence of political and economic circumstances produced by the World War I and its aftermath. VIAG was created in 1923 at the request of the Treasury Ministry (*Reichsschatzministerium*), which had been responsible for the administration of all state-owned enterprises. Before World War I, the German Reich was not a shareholder in any company; only federal states owned shares in different enterprises. During the war, various companies came close to bankruptcy. For obvious reasons, the Reich offered state loans to those companies, who were producers of essential war material. After the war, many of these companies were still not able to pay back the loans. Finally, the Reich transformed the credits into shares and thus held sizeable shareholdings in a large number of companies. In 1923, the idea arose to build a state-owned holding company by integrating all state-owned enterprises: the VIAG. The ministry planned to introduce private industrial management, thereby rationalising the administration of the individual companies.

During the following decade, VIAG was very busy restructuring the group by selling firms which did not fit into its core businesses and by buying additional companies to support its main industrial branches. The VIAG started off with 86 companies, in which the Reich was the main shareholder.[8] But after a short time, through strategic buying and selling, the 'gigantic grocery' VIAG was transformed into a profit-making, stable group. VIAG focused on four sectors: electricity, aluminium, nitrogen and banking. Though the nitrogen and aluminium subsidiaries suffered heavy fluctuations in the 1920s, systematic inter-group co-operation helped smooth out earnings and increase profitability. Favourable loans from its own bank, the Reichs-Kredit-Gesellschaft, cross-shareholdings, low inter-company prices for electricity and the use of properties helped individual subsidiary firms by improving their balance sheets. The electricity business, the Elektrowerke AG of Berlin, for example, was considered to be of strategic importance and was, therefore, developed systematically in the 1920s by enormous investments of the holding. During Weimar, the state-owned bank, Reichs-Kredit-Gesellschaft, became one of the five biggest Berlin banks. Only the aluminium company, Vereinigte Aluminium-Werke

AG (VAW), and the nitrogen company, Bayerische Stickstoffwerke AG, were not expanding in the same way. Nonetheless, by the early1930s, VIAG had become an enormous and well-functioning group.

The creation of Deutsche Rentenbank-Kreditanstalt (RKA) also dates back to the mid-1920s and was related to the hyperinflation of 1922. The German inflation was stopped by creating a new currency – the 'Deutsche Rentenmark' – issued in 1923 by the newly founded Deutsche Rentenbank.[9] The share capital of the Rentenbank amounted to 3.2 Billion Rentenmark. This amount was raised by mortgaging agricultural and industrial property.[10] The share capital of the Rentenbank was loaned along with 1.2 billion Rentenmark to the Reich. An equal amount was provided to commercial interests, especially the agriculture sector, which received 870-million Rentenmarks in short-term loans at an interest rate of 18 per cent. Along with the price stability successfully implemented in mid-1924, the allies urged the Deutsche Reich to reorganise its currency system and to re-establish the Deutsche Reichsmark, which entailed taking the Rentenmark out of distribution.[11] The liquidation act concerning the Rentenmark was signed on 11 October 1924. The law required that all Rentenmark loans be repaid before the 1 December 1927. This time pressure caused major problems, especially for farmers. It was just the opposite of what the backward German agriculture sector needed to overcome its shortcomings. German efforts to find a reasonable solution to agriculture's precarious financial situation coupled with pressure from Sir Robert Kindersley, the British member of the Dawes Committee, led – after a long and intense discussion – to the founding of the Deutsche Rentenbank-Kreditanstalt in May 1925.[12] Deutsche Rentenbank's funds were transferred to RKA which had the specific task to transform the short-term agricultural loans into medium- or long-term facilities. But the economic crisis in the second half of the 1920s made meeting the needs for new agricultural loans nearly impossible. Even politicians were unwilling to supply RKA with additional funds to manage this crisis. Therefore, RKA was for the first time allowed to issue bonds. In 1926, it issued the Golddiskontbank-bond[13] to the sum of 360 million Reichsmark. During the following two years RKA borrowed nearly USD 130 million from American banks, which enabled the German bank to stabilise the shaky financial situation in agriculture. With its special responsibility to promote agriculture, RKA was not a usual private bank. The question of its ownership is still important for its current successor. Since there were no shares and since the bank was founded by law, i.e., by statute, it did not technically belong to the state or to any shareholder. In some sense, the whole agriculture sector might be considered the owner of this banking institution, as it brought up via the 'Rentenbankgrundschuld' the capital of the Deutsche Rentenbank, which was later transferred to RKA.

THE PARTY AND THE ENTERPRISES

The NSDAP – hindrance or advantage in state-owned enterprises?

With their already-close relationship to the government, state-owned companies were easily brought in line with party policies. It did not take long for the Nazis to get involved in the management of the companies. The impact of the Nazis on the boards of VIAG was extensive; on the boards of RKA nearly total. After 1933, VIAG's supervisory board changed immediately; slowly party members as well as persons well known for their closeness to the Nazis were integrated in the management.[14] This also took place in VIAG's subsidiaries. As early as April 1933, all members of the supervisory board were asked to tender their resignation, but only few members resignations were accepted.[15] The deeper impact on the development of the supervisory board was caused by the unexpected death of its chairman, David Fischer, the former State Secretary of the Finance Ministry, who had headed VIAG's supervisory board since 1926.[16] His replacement was Ernst Trendelenburg, who was not member of the Nazi party, but his closeness to the NS-system was well known.

Power was concentrated among a few people in VIAG's supervisory board. At the centre was Ernst Trendelenburg. During the second half of the 1930s, the supervisory board started to build sub-committees for specific functions such as personnel and financial management. Only a few persons were named in these committees. They built the key figures in the decision making process of the management. The supervisory board ceased to function as a control mechanism run by majority rule. In the 1940s, it rarely even met. Decision-making was limited to a small number of persons, who more and more came from the party.[17]

At this juncture, additional information about the significance of the supervisory board prior to 1945 might be of interest. Compared with today, VIAG's supervisory board (*Aufsichtsrat*) in the first half of this century was more powerful than the management board (*Vorstand*). Therefore, it is not surprising that the impact of the Nazis was first felt on the supervisory board and only later on the management board. VIAG's management board consisted of two members. Wilhelm Lenzmann, who died in 1935, was, like his colleague, a former civil servant in the Treasury Ministry. He was succeeded by Karl Schirner, the former chairman of the management board of the big steel trust Vereinigte Stahlwerke. Oddly, Schirner claimed that he left Vereinigte Stahlwerke because his old firm was too close to the regime.[18] Why he really chose to join VIAG, which in 1936 – as will be discussed later – was already being run in accordance with National Socialist policies aims, remains an open and interesting question, but beyond the scope of this paper. Nonetheless, it is clear that his nomination to VIAG's management board was 'heartily welcomed' by

Hjalmar Schacht.[19] In 1939, Schirner left VIAG's management board for the position of chairman of Deutsche-Erdöl AG's management board. According to Schimer, his new post was much more interesting than that at VIAG, which accounted for his decision to change jobs.[20] There was some truth in this explanation. At VIAG, the two members of the management board – VIAG never had a chairman – strictly divided financial and operational duties. Whatever the real reason, in both cases there was no hint that party members put Schirner under pressure to leave. This cannot be said of other members of the management board: Edgar Landauer, who like his colleague Lenzmann, held his position since the creation of VIAG. But Landauer was Jewish and, in 1937, was forced to resign from the board. Discussions in the supervisory board showed that none of the board members favoured dismissing Landauer, but by that time organising any opposition seems to have been impossible. It is astonishing, though, that Landauer could keep his position until 1937, since Jewish members of the subsidiary management boards were dismissed as early as 1933. The discussion showed that Landauer had friends, who also helped him to leave Germany and live in Great Britain.

As company politics changed enormously with the change from Fischer's supervisory board leadership to Trendelenburg's, so too the transition from Landauer to Alfred Olscher changed the politics of the management board. Olscher, a supervisory board member since 1932, and deputy chairman and member of the NSDAP since 1934, participated in the Keppler Circle and thus moved into the economic elite of the party. When 'PG Olscher'[21] took over the leading role in the VIAG-board, he implemented party directives as soon as they were received from the Economics Ministry without any supervisory board discussion. Olscher was nominated directly by the Ministry of Finance.[22] For the first time a third member was added to the management board. Otto Neubaur, who worked for VIAG-owned Reichs-Kredit-Gesellschaft since 1927 and who was member of its management board since 1934, was nominated.[23] In 1939, an additional member joined the management board: Erich Heller from the Creditanstalt Wiener-Bankverein. The nomination system for the board posts showed the change in management style. Originally, the holding company, with its two-person management board, was managed as an integrated group. The board members did not come the subsidiaries but from governmental agencies. Now the subsidiaries, especially both banks – Reichs-Kredit-Gesellschaft and Creditanstalt Wiener-Bankverein, were represented in the management board. Only Olscher, as the party's representative, did not come from a subsidiary firm. Paradoxically, the priorities of the party and subsidiaries replaced those of the State as the basis of the management board's decisions.

The most important VIAG subsidiary boards lost many of their members, who were replaced by supporters of the regime or party members.

Many of those who remained were willing political servants of the regime. At VIAG there was little need for new Nazis – with the exception of Edgar Landauer – or for active intervention, since the only two persons with sufficient stature to have opposed them – Wilhelm Lenzmann and David Fischer – died shortly after 1933. Of course, the Reich's authority to issue directives along with the network of party members and regime-supporters already added to the various companies limited the scope of non-compliant managers to resist. The well-known quarrels among agencies over spheres of responsibility, which weakened the entire economic system during the Third Reich, occurred frequently at RKA.

Agency Conflicts in Public Institution

Nazi terror against agricultural associations started relatively early. As early as 20 March 1933, Andreas Hermes, president of the '*Raiffeisen-Verband*', an agrarian association, and member of the supervisory board of RKA since 1927, was unjustly imprisoned. Walther Darré, minister of agriculture took over his position at the association. Also, the agricultural cooperatives (*Genossenschaften*) were immediately brought into line with the party by Darré's threatening tirade during a meeting of the cooperatives' advisory board.[24] Darré also quickly moved to establish control over the third agricultural association, the '*Reichslandbund*'. Its president, Graf von Kalckreuth, like Andreas Hermes, was removed from the RKA supervisory board.

After Darré stripped power from the agricultural associations, the chairman of Kreditanstalts' advisory board, Wilhelm Lentze, took the initiative. He offered the then Minister of Agriculture, Alfred Hugenberg, the complete '*Gleichschaltung* of the advisory board' and singled out five board members for immediate dismissal. But his compliant attitude did not protect him for long.[25] In November 1933, Lentze himself was forced to give up his post. On 1 November 1933, he resigned his position as chairman of VIAG's supervisory board as well as his position as president of Deutsche Rentenbank. With his successor, Walter Granzow[26], the NS-typical power play between the different persons and authorities took off. Granzow had been Ministerpresident of Mecklenburg-Schwerin and worked in the 'Rasse- und Siedlungshauptamt' of the SS on agricultural questions.[27] He was responsible inside the SS for financing the settlement of SS-men in the countryside. Granzow's nomination as president of RKA's advisory board showed very clearly where Walther Darré wanted to direct funds.

With rare exceptions, the government's representatives on the advisory board were replaced. But there were no changes to the management board: Hermann Kißler, Moritz Lipp and Walter Szagunn have been members in the board since the foundation of RKA in 1925. In 1933, Szagunn had been already a member of the SS, which he joined '*mit frohem Herzen*' –

with a happy heart. But the management board was expanded in 1933: Gerhard Kokotkiewicz entered. He was supposed to be responsible for the regulation of debts – in the new definition of the ideologist Darré, the 'deobligation' of the farmers. He was a supporter, or better, a favourite of the NSDAP.[28] In 1935, a long-term member of the board, Moritz Lipp, left management. His successor, Gustav Wichtermann, was also a party member (since May 1933).[29]

The RKA general assembly *(Anstaltsversammlung)* was completely replaced with only one exception. At the same time, it was reduced from 110 members to 70. All posts were filled from the four main departments of the Reichs Food Estate *(Reichsnährstand)*, which was built up by Walther Darré in the autumn of 1933 after all agricultural associations had been brought into line with party policies. From this perspective, RKA was much more dominated by the party than VIAG. Whereas at VIAG replacement of board members was a gradual process, at RKA the change occurred in one fell swoop. Albeit at different times, both of them were more or less dominated by party members or regime-friendly persons. And both were closely associated with important Reich agencies: VIAG with the 'Four-Year-Plan', and RKA with the Reichs Food Estate as well as the 'Four-Year-Plan'.

It is not only the impact of the NSDAP inside the enterprises that is significant but also the changing responsibility of authorities for the companies, which defined the relationship between state and enterprises. When VIAG was founded the Treasury Ministry was responsible for that company. Since the Weimar Republic was based on democratic principles, Reichstag created an entire committee to oversee VIAG. But this subcommittee of the Reichstag's budget-committee rarely met. In fact, it had absolutely no impact on the strategy or at least the day-to-day affairs of the holding company. In the 1920s, the principal responsibility for VIAG was shifted from the Treasury Ministry to the Ministry of Finance. A short time later, the Economic Ministry began to share responsibility for VIAG with the Ministry of Finance. During the NS-period, the office of the 'Four-Year Plan' gained increasing influence over VIAG. This influence was not so much on the holding company but rather directly on VIAG's individual subsidiaries. This coincided with the 'Four-Year Plan's' organisation of industry into the so-called economic groups (*Wirtschaftsgruppen)* for different sectors. For example, Ludger Westrick, Chairman of VAW, was made head of the economic group 'Leichtmetall' (*Wirtschaftsführer*).

Also in RKA's advisory board there were many representatives of the Reich's authorities, mainly representatives of the ministry of agriculture. Beneath there was a large number of representatives of any kind of agricultural associations and groups. After 1933 RKA was only under the responsibility of the Reich's Food Estate up to the moment, when nutrition became relevant for the warfare and Göring and the 'Four-Year-Plan' started to intervene and claim its responsibility.

THE SIGNIFICANCE OF THESE SECTORS TO THE AUTARKY POLICY

VIAG's Aluminium, Electricity and Nitrogen Activities

The aluminium sector was the most dynamic in the NS-period. Even before the new regime came to power for purely internal economic reasons, VIAG's subsidiaries tried to expand and to rationalize themselves. But after 1933, this quite normal business policy was integrated into Nazi economic planning, especially the plans of Hermann Göring. Göring's strong will to improve and expand the Luftwaffe required increasing amounts of aluminium. VIAG's VAW, with 70 percent of German production, was by far the largest aluminium company and, therefore, perfect for Göring's purposes. Moreover, within the VIAG group, the electricity division was well equipped to guarantee the needed amount of energy for the energy-intense production of aluminium. The systematic expansion of Vereinigte Aluminium-Werke AG (VAW) started in 1934–35.[30] Not only increased orders, but also generous state subsidies, in the form of increase of the share capital and favourable loans, aided this development.[31] In 1936, Germany was already the number one aluminium producer in the world, overtaking the USA in production quantities. Good relations with VAW's Italian and Swiss partners, mainly suppliers of aluminium oxide, made the expansion of this VIAG subsidiary less risky. Even the favourable price VAW gave the State for aluminium had economic benefits. This artificially low price coupled with State subsidies warded off potential VAW competitors. Some smaller firms were driven out of business,[32] paving the way for VAW to monopolise the aluminium sector, a welcome development for both, VIAG and Göring.

With the beginning of the war in 1939, economic life in Germany deteriorated. But contracts with foreign suppliers were still stable. With its special standing inside the NS-economy as a producer of war-relevant material and its good connections with Göring, VAW was able to manage the problem of labour shortage. In the beginning of the war, VAW was granted by the authorities special permission to lengthen working hours, mostly regarding female workers.[33] VAW was also successful in getting back its labour force from the army. VAW was allocated an enormous number of forced labour. In some of the subsidiaries of VIAG, the percentage of foreign labour made up over 50 per cent of the entire workforce.[34] The treatment of the slave labour was inhumane. Though we do not have a lot of documentation on this subject, those that we do have do not paint a nice picture. The way VAW treated its forced labour led Fritz Sauckel, leader of the 'Zwangsarbeitereinsatz', to write several letters to the management of VAW threatening the company to stop further allocation of labour force if VAW continues this kind of treatment.[35]

In addition, directives of the board of management forbidding slave labourers to enter air-raid shelters during an air attack indicated that the responsible managers were willing to risk the lives of these people. Other documents indicate that the chairman of the management board, Ludger Westrick, approved 'making an example of a slave labourer' in order to put a stop to the rising number of escapes from the firm.[36]

Westrick, who did not appear to be a very political Nazi, even though his career at VAW began with the replacement of a Jewish colleague in 1933, was the manager who worked most closely with the 'Four-Year Plan'. He was chairman of the 'Wirtschaftsgruppe Leichtmetall', which was later active in Norway and France.[37] NS-economic policies and the interests of the VAW were virtually identical. The autarky policy created a growing need of aluminium and VAW produced it. VAW often did more than the NS regime required, not only regarding slave labour, but also in its expansion. Even when VAW was producing more aluminium than the armament industry needed – in the 1940s aluminium was used as a substitute for other metals, VAW argued for more State supplies for further investment in productive capacity. Because the Nazis found the State monopoly attractive, VAW received permission for the expansion.

VIAG's main subsidiary in the 1920s – its electricity division – was as important for rearmament and autarky as aluminium, perhaps even more so. The great relevance of cheap energy for the production of aluminium was obvious; the Reich favoured the expansion of the Elektrowerke AG and the other VIAG electricity subsidiaries. The idea of creating a monopoly for Germany's long-term energy needs arose in 1938 with the transfer of the rights to Austrian water-power to VIAG. The competitors of VIAG – RWE, Preussag/VEBA, Bayernwerk – had lost the battle for the rights. The preference for hydroelectric power instead of power generated by coal dated back to the 1920s, when the German electricity sector started to build an integrated grid system. The idea to replace expensive coal-produced energy with cheap water-generated power encouraged the creation of an integrated grid system, which could provide electricity at any time wherever it is needed.[38] Since German water sources were limited and the mountains of Austria an enormous resource, Göring allowed VIAG to use Austrian water-power for the so-called 'Tauernkraftwerk' a gigantic hydroelectric power-plant, which he sponsored.[39] VIAG set up a separate subsidiary, the 'Alpenelektrowerke' to exploit the Austrian water-power. A technical disaster, the project was never able to supply Germany with the enormous amounts of energy urgently needed. Though a few smaller power plants were under construction at the same time, they were finished too late to be of any use in the war effort.

The Austrian expansion, however, led to new ventures for VIAG as well as for the State. VIAG sensed the opportunity to gain a monopoly over the entire energy sector in the medium-term. These plans even succeeded in Germany. The idea of attaining a Reichs-monopoly was followed by a plan to build a Europe-wide grid system, which would connect electricity sources and users from Norway down to Italy, from Russia to Spain, and, of course, into the German grid system. The relevant agencies, especially the 'Generalinspekteur für Energie' under Fritz Todt und Albrecht Speer, supported this idea for post-war Germany. But the government also developed plans to divide the holding company, and to build a new, separate electricity company under the leadership of VIAG's electricity companies.[40]

VIAG's third division also tried to expand, but it was less successful than the others, as the nitrogen business was dominated by IG Farben.[41] Ironically, VIAG was hindered in this sector by the same system that was helping it in the others. It adopted a strategy of co-operation with IG Farben, which led to the transformation of the Bayerische Kraftwerke AG into a joint venture Süddeutsche Stickstoffwerke AG (SKW), with a 30 per cent share holding by IG Farben. VIAG had hoped to gain more technical information from the IG, but the giant chemical company knew how to prevent this transfer. VIAG tried in vain to re-gain Farben's 30 per cent holding. Because of this failure, SKW played only a minor role in VIAG's future plans.[42]

In conclusion, VIAG was indeed very successful, but the character of the holding company had changed completely. The strength of VIAG in the 1920s and the early 1930s was its integrated group structure. The responsible authorities *treated* VIAG as one big company and dealt *directly* with the head of the group. During the Nazi era, the VIAG holding company lost its importance. The individual subsidiaries attained more power and influence. In the 1920s, the group's main advantage was its ability to evaluate the economic shortcomings of its subsidiary firms. This strength vanished. The holding company was only used for very limited purposes. Göring was interested in the individual companies and in creating monopolies. Business, such as the allocating of labour or of state finance, was done directly between the government and the subsidiaries.

There was less scope for the management board of VIAG to intervene. The forced sale of subsidiary firms and the construction of individual plants that were strategic for the war effort but had little or no economic benefit, without consulting the holding company, evidenced this development. On the other hand – and I would like to stress this point – the chairmen of the individual companies adhered to business policies that far exceeded the expectations of the state. In the end, the VIAG group became the 'plaything' of the 'Four-Year Plan'. Placing managers sympathetic to party aims in key positions had already reduced to a minimum the scope of independent company action. But in hopes of insuring a bright, stable future for themselves, the chairmen of the individual firms sometimes exceeded the NS-regime's directives. Economically, the state giant did not have any worries: it needed no foreign markets. Its divisions were very important for armament production, which guaranteed sales, at least in the short run. Aluminium was sold to the air force; nitrogen was urgently needed for agricultural production, and insatiable demand for electricity paved the way for future economic successes.

Agriculture

As discussed, RKA was founded in the 1920s to provide agriculture with necessary medium- and long-term financing. Its primary mission was to re-structure the 1923 short-term credits into medium- or long-term facilities backed by the income earned by the *Rentenbankgrundschuld*, the amount every farmer had to pay for his property, and by State capital. Soon after 1933, with Darrés's successful seizure of power, the politics of lending money changed radically. Loans were granted for the storage of agricul-tural products and for increasing productivity with questionable benefits and in which the individual farmers no longer played a role. With increas-ing labour shortages, which hit agriculture early because industry salaries were higher, political slogans changed quickly. Rationalisation, automati-sation and the expansion of arable land took on greater importance, resulting in new measures for granting loans. The bank itself had less influence on lending because state law determined the conditions. But from an agrarian point of view, these new measures for increasing produc-tivity were not always economically sensible. Also granting individual loans to the end creditor was rarely determined by RKA, as it was only a refinancing institution, which forwarded loans to other banks or other institutions for certain purposes defined by law. The other banks actually granted the loans to individual farmers. During the Nazi era, the many procedures for granting loans were established by the so-called 'Kreisbauernführer' (leader of farmers for a district), who also controlled the forced economy (*Zwangsbewirtschaftung*).

Since the founding of RKA, its activities were concentrated on reducing the financial pressures caused by the short-term loans with high interest rates (up to 18 per cent) by converting those loans into medium- or long-term facilities. But with the new law of 1933, the so-called 'Erbhofgesetz' (Estate Inheritance Law) reflected the new Nazi focus: Darré wanted the complete relief of the farmers' debts and thus this law forbid the farmers to create new debts. This idea of a debtless agriculture remained utopian. In 1933, the total amount of agricultural debt amounted to 14 billion RM. As late as 1943, only eleven to twelve per cent of German farms were debt free (about 75,000 farms), and the rate of new debt accumulation had already begun to increase in 1936/37. Through 1937, the amount of the so-called 'transition loans' was also increasing at RKA, when they vanished in their original form from RKA's balance sheet. They were not paid back, but rather the 'Erbhofgesetz' required that the management board re-classify the RM 50.2 million in loans to the so-called 'different-mortgage-loans' account. Officially, they no longer existed, which was in line with Walter Darré's ideological intentions.

Once Darré had the whole agriculture sector under the control of the 'Reichs Food Estate', he found RKA the perfect instrument to finance his ideology of 'Blood and Soil' (Blut und Boden-Ideologie). His concept of the 'Erbhof' – estate inheritance – apart from the usual racist ideology, called for debt-free farmers with guaranteed sales at fixed prices all under strict control of and financed by RKA. This worked perfectly well until economic pressures caused by the autarky policies thrust Göring onto centre stage. The conflicting priorities of Darrés' 'Blood and Soil' and Göring's 'combat for production' (Erzeugungsschlacht) concepts were fought out in the bank: SS-man Granzow – brother in law of Goebbels and a friend of Darré – followed the ideals of Darré without question. Already in 1934, when Schacht created his 'New Plan', which required greater agricultural production, Hermann Kissler, still chairman of the management board, saw an opportunity of restoring the original terms of the agrarian credits. The management board argued that greater production would require removing the prohibition on new debts for the farmers, which had been introduced by Darrés's 'Erbhofgesetz'. Only further loans would allow agriculture to make a contribution to the 'combat for productivity'. Darré's policies lost their influence with a 'decree of the leader' (Führererlaß), which transferred responsibility for agriculture from Darré's Ministry of Agriculture to the office of the 'Four-Year Plan'.

Inside the management board, Szagunn was responsible for the implementation of Göring's plans to promote productivity. Immediately after changing the control of RKA, the bank received 40 million RM from the state budget to improve productivity. This was loaned to the farmers at an interest rate of two per cent.

This transfer of control was important for RKA. It was the result of Granzow's efforts to reduce Darré's power. Granzow had suggested to Göring that he should appoint Herbert Backe, Darré's state secretary and Granzow's colleague in RKA's supervisory board, minister of agriculture.[43] Granzow, who had up to this time supported Darré's policies without question, now tried to play his own game. But he became the victim of his own intrigue. Göring decided – after a meeting with Himmler and Hitler about this staffing – to keep Darré in his position. Since his intriguing was now known, Granzow increasingly lost power, a victim of the well-known NS-quarrels amoung ministries and agencies that paralysed the government.

In the aftermath of this political bickering, the configuration of power within RKA's supervisory board was reshuffled. Backe became the central figure. He also headed the 'Business group for food' within the organisation of the 'Four-Year-Plan', which added to his power. Changes in the relative power of individuals were evident when Szagunn unexpectedly died in 1937, opening a position on the board. As rumours circulated that the management board would soon fill his post, Darré contacted Granzow directly to tell him that only Backe was empowered to determine who would succeed Szagunn. In the end, no one was appointed to the board seat.

This fight among leading Nazis allowed the management board, especially Kissler, to push the development of agrarian credits along economic rather than political lines. Several attempts by the SS to get financial support for the settlement of SS-men, for example, were rebuffed with the justification that this kind of financing was not RKA's responsibility. The bank also refused to finance the settlement of Germans in East Europe. These decisions were less politically motivated than a reflection of the board's strict adherence to what it perceived as its primary mission.[44] To sum up, the Nazis dominated RKA's general assembly, supervisory board and even the board of management.

After Darré and his friends gained power in the bank, the future for agriculture and the agrarian credits changed completely. In the long run, the individual farmer would have been reduced to a firm supported by the state and only being able to exist with this support. Fixed prices, fixed production and sales would have eliminated any vestiges of a free market. Not only that the agriculture would have changed its face in that way, also the agrarian credit was planned to vanish. It was even intended by some that the bank would be dissolved as soon as all farmers were debt free. The management board's measure to keep the agrarian credit system running were at times nearly illegal but helped to reduce the harm that aspects of NS ideology might have done to German agriculture. On the other hand, of course, by keeping this credit system functional, the bank helped the Nazis by improving food production. Regarding the failure of planning to solve the general problem of Germany's nutritional needs during the war, the support of German farmers was particularly important in light of Göring's failure to develop Polish and later Ukrainian production sufficiently.

CONCLUSION AND OUTLOOK

There are two conclusions which can be drawn from this paper: One is to state the existence of systems. Both of the enterprises discussed turned out to be under strong, direct control of the Reichs' agencies, at least of the

Four-Year Plan. The authorities had plans for the enterprises, which created limits on the companies' activities. But in both enterprises there was a
degree of freedom for planning and implementation that depended on the
individuals involved. In the end the decision making process was more
dominated by men then by systems or institutional forces.

VIAG's economic strategy was consistent with the Nazis plans, especially with Göring's economic aims. Moreover, VIAG was able to use its
good relationship with the Reich against its competitors and to gain a lot
of advantages for its economic development. But VIAG was later reduced
to a 'plaything' of the State. This should have been no surprise; most of the
leaders at VIAG were Nazis. But not all of managers of subsidiaries were
party-members or friends of the party. Nevertheless, some of these managers turned out to be more NS-strategic then others. Their overwhelming
desire to form monopolies in their sectors with the help of the government
seemed to seduce managers to co-operate. They, too, had some freedom of
action, but as was the case with VAW, the scope of management freedom
was sometimes used to do more not less than Göring asked. The RKA
managers exploited the quarrels between Darré's and Göring's representatives, but sometimes, as Kissler did, to save their own pet projects. The
histories of both companies illustrate the temptation of government officials to treat state enterprises as their personal trinkets, to be used and
even disposed of when it seemed opportune for the Reich and the Nazis.

As this paper argues that the decision-making processes became more
and more dominated by men rather than by systems and institutions, it is
appropriate to say something of the post-war histories of some of the
individuals involved. Ernst Trendelenburg, chairman of the VIAG supervisory board, committed suicide in the last days of the war. Alfred Olscher,
the chairman of VIAG's management board, died during his Russian imprisonment. Erich Heller, also member of VIAG's management board,
vanished. Last seen in Austria. According to oral testimony that I received,
Walter Granzow also seems to have died shortly after the war. Hermann
Kissler kept his position as chairman of RKA and its successor,
Landwirtschaftliche Rentenbank, up to the late 1950s. Some of his colleagues were dismissed but later received other positions in German business.

Ludger Westrick, chairman of VAW's management board, VIAG's aluminium division, was imprisoned by the Russian Army. According to some
rumours, his wife took care of some Russian soldiers and, after their
return to the Red Army, Westrick was released. There may also be another
explanation for why Westrick was not prosecuted after the war. Interrogation reports in the National Archives in Washington showed that his name
had been changed to Westring. When Göring was asked about Westring's
activities, Göring first said no, then that he was not sure, and finally that

he did not want to comment.[45] In any case, the issue was dropped and Westrick stayed at his post. He became trustee of VIAG and ended his career as state secretary in the Economics Ministry under minister Ludwig Erhard.

The liquidation of RKA started in 1949 with the creation of a new bank for refinancing agricultural debt, the Landwirtschaftliche Rentenbank, and ended in 1978.

VIAG had severe problems after the war, which resulted in its privatisation in 1986. With the merger of VIAG and VEBA, another former state-owned enterprise – owned by the Prussian State in the NS-period and a firm that was also privatised step by step beginning in the 1950s – VIAG's independent history will soon come to an end. With some historical irony, after a long period of diversification, the merger of these companies will bring them back to their roots, their old strengths of electricity and chemistry. The merged company will keep a third segment, VIAG's cellular net. The name VIAG in 2000 became history too, when the merged company is re-christened 'E.on'.

Finally, to return to the initial question, were state-owned enterprises Hitler's willing servants, we can say as institutions the answer is definitely yes. But behind this general statement, we find a myriad of details illustrating a wide-range of different kinds of behaviour ranging from efforts to resist the regime to blatant exploitation of companies' privileged circumstances. The Nazi system forced enterprises to co-operate, but individuals had some influence on how and when that co-operation was implemented.

NOTES

1. This paper was given in various forms at several colloquia: '*Unternehmen* im Nationalsozialismus' held at 2–3 June, 1999 at the Humboldt-University in Berlin, at the colloqium of Prof. Peter Hayes at the Northwestern University in Evanstone, Illinois, in November 1999 and at the colloqium of Prof. Gerald D. Feldman at the University of California at Berkeley in March 2000. I would like to thank the participants for their useful comments on the paper. I sincerely appreciate the time and effort Prof. Christopher Kobrak took in refining this paper for publication.

2. The VIAG was 100 per cent state owned. It was created by forming a group of Elektrowerke AG, Reichs-Kredit-Gesellschaft AG, Vereinigte Aluminium Werke AG and Deutsche Werke AG. The state transferred the 100 per cent shares of all these companies to VIAG. Thus these companies were transferred to subsidiaries of VIAG. Additionally the state transferred all shares of different companies to the holding company VIAG.

3. The history of VIAG is presented in Manfred Pohl/Andrea H. Schneider, *VIAG Aktiengesellschaft, Vom Staatsunternehmen zum internationalen Konzern*, München 1998.

4. The Rentenbank-Kreditanstalt was a public institution. Since it did not have

shares it was not owned by anyone. Since it is ruled by law, at least it has to be defined as public. The foundation and the development of the Rentenbank-Kreditanstalt is provided in Manfred Pohl/Andrea H. Schneider, *Die Rentenbank, Von der Rentenmark zur Förderung der Landwirtschaft*, München 1999.

5. Horst Gies, 'Aufgaben und Probleme der nationalsozialistischen Ernährungswirtschaft 1933–1939', in: *VSWG* (1979), p. 466–99.

6. Eberhard Kolb, *Die Weimarer Republik*, München 1993.

7. For further information on the autarky policy and the means to realize it see Dieter Petzina, *Autarkiepolitik im Dritten Reich. Der nationalsozialistische Vierjahresplan*, Stuttgart 1948 and Richard Overy, *Goering, The 'Iron Man'*, London 1984.

8. Beneath the four main enterprises – Deutsche Werke AG, Elektrowerke AG, Vereinigte Aluminium Werke AG and Reichs-Kredit-Gesellschaft AG – were a wide range of different subsidiaries, among these were a telephone company (Telephon-Fabrik AG), a paper-producing enterprise (AG für Pappenfabrikation), a fishing company (Deutsche Fischerei AG), a ship transport firm (Schlesische Dampfer-Compagnie-Berliern Lloyd and a producer of butter (Flensburger Margarinewerke GmbH).

9. For the inflation see Gerald D. Feldman, *The Great Disorder. Politics, Economics, and Society in the German Inflation, 1914–1924*, Oxford 1993 and Carl-Ludwig Holtfrerich, *Die deutsche Inflation 1914–1924. Ursachen und Folgen in internationaler Perspektive*, Berlin/New York 1980.

10. This amount – the so called '*Rentenbankgrundschuld*' ('Rentenbanks' mortgage') – was collected via tax offices.

11. The allies agreed on the so called 'Dawes-plan', which contained the demand to restart the function of the central bank.

12. Especially the intervention of the competitor in the agrarian credit system – the Preußische Zentralgenossenschaftskasse (the bank of the agrarian cooperatives) – caused long-lasting discussions in the German parliament. Also the differing interpretation of the whole procedure by the directory of the Reichsbank lengthened the process of creation. See correspondence in: Bundesarchiv Berlin, R3101/16491 and minutes of the Reichstag and Reichstagsdrucksachen.

13. The Golddiskontbank was one of the three parallel existing German central banks in 1924: the Reichsbank, issuing a paper currency and trying to keep the value stable. The Deutsche Rentenbank issuing valuable banknotes and the Golddiskontbank which was founded on Pound Sterling. The latter never issued its own banknotes, but its goldbonds were separated in coupons which circulated in the public like money. See Harold James, 'Die Reichsbank 1876 bis 1945', in: Deutsche Bundesbank (ed.), *Fünfzig Jahre Deutsche Mark. Notenbank und Währung in Deutschland seit 1948*, München 1998, p. 29–89, here p. 53 f.

14. There remained David Fischer, Richard Damm, Gustav Hammer, Hermann Jahncke, Paul Kempner, Florian Klöckner, Alfred Olscher, Reinhold Georg Quaatz, Franz Schroeder, Konrad Sterner and Franz Urbig. Newly nominated were Paul Bang, Christian Otto Fischer, Ewald Hecker, Johannes

Heintze, Wilhelm Koeppel, Max von der Porten und Albert Vögler. See Business Reports of VIAG 1933–45, in: VIAG archives.

15. Some well-known industrialists – for example, Max von der Porten, Chairman of the VAW's Management Board – were dismissed, because he was Jewish.

16. Fischer suceeded Heinrich Albert, after his dismissal caused by the Deutsche Werke scandal in the mid 1920s. More details see Pohl/Schneider, *VIAG Aktiengesellschaft*, p. 41–47.

17. This was a small number of members of the supervisory board, especially Trendelenburg and Olscher. See protocols of the supervisory board, in: VIAG archives.

18. Typed manuscript of Karl Schirner from 19 November 1946, privately owned by the Schirner family.

19. See protocol of the supervisory board meeting of 10 July 1935, *Historical Archive of Deutsche Bank*, Franz Urbig.

20. See protocol and attachments of the supervisory board meeting of 12 May 1938, *Historical Archive of Deutsche Bank*, Franz Urbig.

21. PG means member of the party (*Parteigenosse*).

22. There was no discussion or nominiation inside the boards of RKA. See correspondence Ministry of Finance to Supervisory Board of VIAG and Reichs-Kredit-Gesellschaft of 19 March 1937, *Historical Archive of Deutsche Bank*, Franz Urbig.

23. Interestingly, Otto Neubaur was chairman of the management board of the Kreditanstalt für Wiederaufbau in post-war Germany. Beginning in 1940, he served in the military at the front. See 'Business Reports of VIAG 1940' f., *VIAG archives*.

24. See Horst Gies, 'Die nationalsozialistische Machtergreifung auf dem agrarpolitischen Sektor', in: *Zeitschrift für Agrargeschichte und Agrarsozialogie*, 1968, p. 210–232.

25. Lentze to Reichsrat from 10 May 1933, Bundesarchiv Berlin, R2/31044.

26. Granzow was born on 13 August 1887 in Schönhagen, Brandenburg. In his interrogation, he admitted his close relation to Darré, Himmler and Göring. See 'Preliminary Interrogation Report, PIR 20': National Archives, Washington, RG 165/390/35/07/05, Box 657.

27. Gustavo Corni/Horst Gies, *Brot, Butter, Kanonen. Die Ernährungswirtschaft in Deutschland unter der Diktatur Hitlers*, Berlin 1997.

28. So Heinrich Schmidkowski, an former employee of RKA, said during an interview held by the author on the 14 October, 1998.

29. See Berlin Document Centre, Bundesarchiv Berlin.

30. In 1936, the production of aluminium was already five times higher than in 1933.

31. See protocols of the supervisory board meetings: VIAG archives.

32. Attachment to the letter of VAW to ministry of finance from 25 June 1937, in: Bundesarchiv Berlin, R2/17624 and Business Reports, in: VIAG archives.

33. See Pr.Br.Rep. 43, Cottbus, 35, in: Brandenburgisches Landeshauptarchiv, Postdam and Pr.Br.Rep. 75, VAW Lautawerk, no. 36 and no. 13, in: Brandenburgisches Landeshauptarchiv, Postdam.

34. See ibid.
35. See Pr.Br.Rep. 75, VAW Lautawerk, in: Brandenburgisches Landeshauptarchiv, Potsdam.
36. See Pr.Br.Rep. 75, VAW Lautawerk, in: Brandenburgisches Landeshauptarchiv, Potsdam.
37. See interrogation report of Göring from 2 June 1945, in: RG 260/390/44/44/ 03, Box 630, File 4, NARA-Gov, Washington, and documentation in: Bundesarchive Berlin, R2/17624.
38. In 1935, the 'law for the promotion of the electricity economy' laid out the basic rules for this sector. It called for the regional division of Germany, with one main provider for each region: RWE in the West, Preussag in the North, EWAG in Central and East Germany, and Bayernwerk in the South. The numerous small producers and providers were dramatically obstacled by this new law.
39. Protocol of the supervisory board meeting of 23 September 1938: VIAG archives.
40. The plans of the 'Reichssammelschiene' are published in Pohl/Schneider, VIAG Aktiengesellschaft. See diverse correspondence of the Reichskanzlei, Finance Ministry and bulletins, in: Bundearchiv Berlin, R2/17663 and re- marks of Olscher regarding the 'Reichsspitze' of 23 August 1941, in: VIAG archives. The dealings with the authorities are also mentioned by Olscher at the meeting of the supervisory board on the 10 May 1938, in: VIAG archives.
41. Peter Hayes, Industry and Ideology, IG Farben in the Nazi Era, Cambridge 1987.
42. Documention in: VIAG archives.
43. Another major player at this time was Reichsobmann Wilhelm Meinberg, who was also integrated in the network of the Reich's Food Estate. Granzow wanted him to head the Reich's Food Estate, replacing Darré, who would be pushed into another position.
44. This was the Deutsche Siedlungsbank. The task of settling financial claims in agriculture originally rested with RKA, but RKA lost its responsibility in that field to the new bank.
45. Interrogation report of Goering from 2 June, 1945, in: NARA-Gov., Wash- ington, RG 260: 390/44/33/03, Box 630, File 4.

For Product Safety Concerns and Information please contact our EU
representative GPSR@taylorandfrancis.com Taylor & Francis Verlag GmbH,
Kaufingerstraße 24, 80331 München, Germany

Printed and bound by CPI Group (UK) Ltd, Croydon, CR0 4YY
01/05/2025
01858331-0002